EFFICIENCY
SWIMMING

EFFICIENCY SWIMMING

Gene R. Hagerman
with
John W. Atkins
John G. McMurtry
J. Richard Steadman, M.D.

Illustrated by Lane Dupont

BANTAM BOOKS

TORONTO · NEW YORK · LONDON · SYDNEY · AUCKLAND

EFFICIENCY SWIMMING
A Bantam Book / July 1987

Library of Congress Cataloging-in-Publication Data
Hagerman, Gene R.
Efficiency swimming.

  Bibliography: p. 139
  1. Swimming—Training. 2. Swimming—Physiological aspects. I. Atkins,
John W.
GV837.3.E33 1987 797.2'1 86-47903
ISBN 0-553-34413-7

Published simultaneously in the United States and Canada

PRINTED IN THE UNITED STATES OF AMERICA

CW   0 9 8 7 6 5 4 3 2 1

ACKNOWLEDGMENTS

This series of books would not have been written without the patience and support of Janet Nelson, and our editor, Tobi Sanders. A big thank you to Inez Aimee for organizing the project. An important thank you to Gay, Ciska, and Bobbi. Finally, we would like to thank all athletes both recreational and elite who have played a very important role in the authors' lives.

CONTENTS

INTRODUCTION

The idea of this book began in 1982. At that time the U.S. Ski Team was beginning its final push toward the Winter Olympics in Sarajevo, Yugoslavia. John Atkins was the trainer for the Women's Team and John McMurtry was their slalom and giant slalom coach. These two formed a unique team combining the knowledge of a trainer in the area of sports performance, with the coach's emphasis on technique. At that time, a third element was added to the formula, Gene "Topper" Hagerman, an exercise physiologist. As chairman of the medical group of the U.S. Ski Team I was able to watch these three work together, designing sport-specific training programs that would be used to enhance the athlete's performance.

I had felt for many years that proper training would not only improve performance but also help prevent injuries. A graduated exercise program was developed that emphasized not only the classical training in strength and power, but also sport-specific endurance exercises. These two elements combined with sensible nutrition rounded out our approach to optimum athletic performance.

Dr. Hagerman brought a unique talent to the program. He had worked as a sports physiologist for the Olympic Training Center at Squaw Valley and later at Colorado Springs, Colorado. In this capacity he had examined, tested, and given definitive advice on training to most of the great amateur athletes in the country. His familiarity with *all* of the amateur sports included in the Olympics, and his personal contact with the highest level individual athletes gave him a unique understanding for the needs of each sport, and allowed him to catalog their similarities from a physiological stand-point. It was this special expertise that Topper brought to the U.S. Ski Team.

During the next two years we worked together to help create a sports medicine program that emphasized specificity of training, injury prevention, mental toughness, and careful rehabilitation when injuries occurred.

A common bond existed between the four of us and we worked together, sharing ideas, and developing concepts that we hoped would prove valid by the results at Sarajevo. Those two years preceding the Olympics our primary interest focused on condition-ing the athletes for skiing. In order to prepare we had to refamiliarize ourselves with all sports and plug in specific exercises from each, which would correlate best with skiing. As this work progressed, I became increasingly aware of the lack of availability of this information to the sports-minded public. If the highest level ath-letes could improve their performance with our approach, it seems that recreational athletes could benefit even more. At Sarajevo, the U.S. Ski Team became the U.S. Olympic Team for a two-week period. During this time our athletes compete for and represent the United States. It is during a competition such as this that concepts are proven or discarded. The U.S. Olympic Ski Team proved we were right. Although our contribution was only part of the reason for the U.S.'s success, no athlete in the world was better conditioned, trained, or prepared for competition than the U.S. Alpine Ski Team.

Five medals—three gold and two silver—were won. For Amer-ica, this was an achievement comparable to Switzerland winning the Super Bowl, Sweden winning the World Series, or Liechtenstein winning the NBA play-offs.

This confirmed, for me, that our contribution to the competitive edge was important, and that our research could benefit all ath-letes or aspiring athletes, recreational or world class.

The first step in achieving this goal was to bring the group together formally. This resulted in the formation of the S.P.O.R.T., Inc. (Sports Performance Orthopedic Rehabilitation and Training) Group. For two years after the Olympics, we researched any new information that became available in sports and consolidated our approach. Then we were ready. We put together this group of books on efficiency in sports based on the concept that recreational and competitive athletics enhance our enjoyment of life and can be beneficial to health maintenance as well as our self-esteem. Through this series of books, S.P.O.R.T., Inc. is providing world class information to all levels of athletics.

—Richard Steadman, M.D.

CHAPTER 1
TRAINING STEPS

Every athlete knows it takes more than a series of movements to get from one point to another, reach a height, or perform a maneuver. Each sport consists of a multiplicity of coordinated and simultaneous actions using the arms, legs, hands, feet, torso, and head.

The head, in fact, is the most important part of the anatomy involved in any sport, particularly at the higher levels of skill and achievement. Elite athletes the world over use their minds as much as their bodies in learning to perfect their techniques as well as in planning and preparing to compete. They think through their physical requirements, training regimen, nutritional needs, injury prevention and rehabilitation, and psychological orientation.

In addition to knowing their training needs and understanding their anatomical abilities, top athletes also have systematic, structured programs to build up and maintain their best possible physical condition. They are *efficient* athletes; they use *efficient* methods to get to the top of their sport; they stay in peak physical condition by maintaining an *efficient* training program.

Such elite athletes have many opportunities to learn to be efficient in their training. They may have coaches or trainers who provide them with the basic methods to become efficient; they may pick up ideas from extensive reading about their sport, or they may simply make the effort to devise a system themselves. Whatever the source of an elite athlete's training and fitness program, few recreational or even advanced amateur athletes have access to those efficient methods.

Sharing Knowledge

With that in mind, S.P.O.R.T., Inc. decided it was time to share the secrets of efficient training with ordinary people who want to improve their sports performance. S.P.O.R.T., Inc., which stands for Sports, Performance, Orthopedic, Research, and Training, is a corporation founded by four men who collectively have spent over fifty years coaching, training, and caring for athletes who compete at the highest international level.

The four men worked with the United States Alpine Ski Team in the early 1980s and through the 1984 Winter Olympics, in which U.S. skiers won three gold and two silver medals. The sports training backgrounds of S.P.O.R.T., Inc., however, go far beyond skiing.

- John Atkins has a master's degree in physical education and an athletic training certificate from the University of Utah. He was head trainer of the Women's Alpine Ski Team for seven years and has also worked with athletes at the college level and with professional football stars.
- Topper Hagerman has a Ph.D. in exercise physiology from Ohio State University. Before becoming the trainer for the Men's Alpine Ski Team in 1982, he headed the Sports Physiology Laboratory at the United States Olympic Committee Training Centers in Squaw Valley, California, and Colorado Springs, Colorado, where he worked with athletes in many fields.
- John McMurtry has a master's degree in exercise science from Denver University. He served with the United States Alpine Ski Team for eight years and was head women's coach in slalom and giant slalom from 1980 to 1984, when the women's team turned in their most outstanding performances.
- Richard Steadman, M.D., received his medical degree from the University of Texas–Southwestern in Dallas. He has been chief of the United States Alpine Ski Team Sports Medicine Program for ten years. He is an internationally recognized orthopedic surgeon, well known for his progressive rehabilitation and conditioning programs.

Since 1984, the four men as employees of S.P.O.R.T., Inc. have worked together in South Lake Tahoe, California. In this unique venture, they have helped numerous athletes and nonathletes in rehabilitation and fitness regimens following surgery. They also developed the S.P.O.R.T. Cord, an exercise device made of surgical tubing (see chapter 2), which can be used almost anywhere to supplement conventional exercise programs for athletes of all abilities. S.P.O.R.T., Inc. also conducts fitness vacation sessions in Hawaii and international ski tours in Europe.

This broad experience convinced S.P.O.R.T., Inc. that athletes at any level can improve if they know the guidelines and have cohesive plans to get all the parts of training working together. That is the goal of this book. It is a practical guide to the uses of sports physiology, training equipment, biomechanics, injury prevention and care, nutrition, and basic psychology aimed at helping swimmers swim better.

That goal—swimming better—obviously varies according to inherent ability and can range from the efforts of a beginner trying to change paddling into smooth strokes to an expert's attempts to gain speed for competition. Athletes of every ability level can create training regimens to fit their individual needs. The most important aspect of building a training program is the interaction of the parts—physiology, biomechanics, nutrition, psychology, and all the other aspects—with the strokes. A coordinated approach is at the heart of *Efficiency Swimming*.

Notes on Training Needs

Professional athletes know that the most difficult part of training is maintaining desire. Without the desire to train, there can be no driving force, no discipline, no deep-felt need to improve. Modern life has so many other attractions, interests, and distractions that it is easy to forgo the workouts that are essential to reaching a goal of efficient swimming.

A proven way to overcome the temptation to avoid training is to continually reinforce the need to maintain a training regimen. *Identifying who, what, why, when, where, and how you train can provide that essential reinforcement to continue training.* Following are some explanations for the five *W*s and an *H*, but each swimmer should add his or her own ideas and reasons for training.

Who. This is the individual athlete attempting to accomplish a personal goal. The goal may be a conquest or a personal challenge, but its accomplishment can make the most elementary swimmer feel like an Olympic champion.

What. This is a visual image of the goal an athlete expects to achieve from the training program. It is the focus of the workouts.

Why. This defines the benefits an athlete expects from training. The physical rewards are apparent; the psychological rewards are more subtle and usually come more slowly.

When. This is determined by an athlete's internal schedule as well as external priorities. Some people like a morning swim program and find that it sets them up for other activities. Others prefer evening workouts because they feel more energetic at that time of day. Whatever the situation, planning the *"when"* is as vital as the actual performance of the training activities.

Where. This, of course, depends on the facilities available. But serious trainees will try to live, work, or go to school close to appropriate training facilities. With the growing popularity of health centers, workout equipment is more readily available than in the past.

How. This depends on what an athlete wants to accomplish, in what period of time, and on the actual ability of the individual. A goal that is set too high will soon produce discouragement rather than accomplishment.

The Fitness Ladder

Before anyone can swim efficiently, he or she needs to become generally fit. This means applying all the procedures mentioned above as well as acquiring and practicing proper swimming stroke techniques. Most important, becoming fit is like climbing a ladder—one step follows another to the top.

Most people start learning to swim with the crawl stroke and the backstroke, practicing them over short distances. It may take weeks to master these strokes, but gradually as technique improves, so does efficiency.

Many swimmers who are self-taught (even some who have been coached) have acquired bad habits that interfere with efficient swimming. These habits must be corrected before there can be any progress toward efficiency—no matter how much an athlete trains or practices strokes, he or she cannot improve with poor technique.

At these early stages of a fitness program, efficient technique is far more important than speed, power, or swimming long distances. At the same time, as the strokes become easier during this building period, practice sessions can become monotonous. This is the time to alter a training program, to add variety without diminishing the initial goal of perfection (or near-perfection) in technique. For instance, a swimmer can use intervals or repeats with rest periods, instead of straight duration swimming. Intervals and repeats are a type of training using shorter, prescribed distances with a rest or light activity between each interval/repeat. Gradually speed can be built by increasing the rate of arm turnover, adding a more powerful stroke movement throughout the pull, and increasing the rate and power of kicks.

At the same time as strokes are improving, an athlete increases cardiovascular and muscle functions. This, in turn, allows for

INDIVIDUAL EVENTS FOR SWIMMING COMPETITION

Event (meters)	Freestyle	Backstroke	Breaststroke	Butterfly	Individual Medley (all four strokes)
50	X	X	X	X	
100	X	X	X	X	
200	X	X	X	X	X
400	X				X
800	X				
1,500	X				

more intensity in workouts, although the amount of time spent in training remains the same. At this point, some athletes increase the number of workout sessions, but most add new strokes to their repertoire. When learning a new stroke, most swimmers practice it before or after their regular workout sessions. As they become more skilled, they add the stroke to their workout sessions, making sure that technique is correct.

The four strokes used in competitive swimming, along with varied distances, can provide swimmers in training with a way to measure their workout sessions. As technique and physical condition improve, swimming a race distance may give the individual new understanding of and appreciation for all competition.

Swimming in competition requires a high level of fitness and perfect swimming technique, but, win or lose, it can produce great personal satisfaction.

The Training Pyramid

For both recreational and competitive swimmers, training programs should be ongoing. There are, of course, training variations at different skill levels, such as the number of times a swimmer works out per week, the length of the workout sessions, and how hard the individual works out in each session. But frequency, duration, and intensity of training are only three aspects of an entire universe of training variables, all of which make up a huge training pyramid. Efficient swimming is the capstone of that pyramid.

An athlete can visualize the training pyramid as a collection of many small triangles including such variables as endurance, technique, flexibility, strength, energy, sprints, distance, and self-discipline. Each small triangle is a piece of the larger pyramid that makes an athlete efficient. When the parts fit together as perfectly as possible, without gaps, an athlete is achieving a personal peak performance goal. This is the total body approach to training, to exercise, and to competition.

The results of a well-built training pyramid are particularly evident in swimming, because this is among the few sports that combine the use of both upper and lower torso muscles for dynamic output. Performing a swimming stroke over a period of time requires muscular strength, power, and endurance. While the body is being propelled through the water, muscles are being stimulated to get stronger and improve in tone. In conjunction with these muscle activities, cardiovascular benefits are realized throughout exercise sessions. The heart, lungs, and blood flow

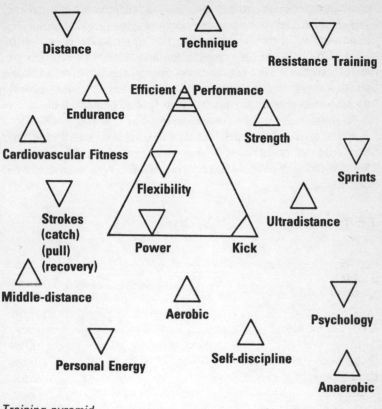

Training pyramid

adapt and operate more efficiently to withstand increased levels of activity. As the body works harder and longer, there is a need to replenish body energy (6 to 14 calories are burned per minute during workout sessions). Proper nutrition combined with exercise influences such body functions as weight loss, energy supplies, and muscle development. All of these components affect resistance to injury, and injury, in turn, can actually be treated through rehabilitation in the liquid environment of water. The entire body is used in the creation of the giant pyramid that results in efficient swimming.

Fitting the pieces together in the training pyramid is, in fact, the essence of efficiency swimming. As a side benefit, this efficiency spills over to other facets of life. The discipline of training sessions and the systematic learning of strokes, kicks, turns, and starts set parameters for time management. The improvement in the cardiovascular and muscular functions of the body permits a greater conservation and better use of energy in daily activities. The maintenance requirements of an athlete's body—proper diet, adequate sleep, energetic workouts—provide an improved product for work, other sports, and social life.

In other words, efficient swimming can positively influence a person's entire way of living. As you learn more about what your body can do, about what fitness feels like, about what you can achieve through physical effort, you will also realize an improved self-image.

CHAPTER 2

SWIMMING EQUIPMENT

To be an efficient swimmer, it makes sense that the most efficient equipment and clothing are necessary, both for the act of swimming itself and for all the training steps leading to the best possible technique. Fortunately, there is an abundance of sophisticated and effective gear available to accomplish this end.

In recent years, manufacturers and designers have analyzed water drag and produced marvels in swimsuits, goggles, and training devices to help swimmers move faster and more easily in

Efficient swimmer

the water. There also has been a growing interest in ways to improve swimming strokes and kicks with in-water training devices. These can help swimmers focus on particular parts of their technique and save time in making improvements. Dryland devices that duplicate actual swimming motions can exercise swimming muscles even when pools or pool time is not available. Resistance training also can add to better functioning and overall fitness. Most of these modern training devices deal with resistance—an opposing or retarding force that must be moved. Other equipment is available to make training more pleasant and interesting, which is very important in helping an athlete maintain a consistent and effective training regimen.

While the need for better equipment at all levels of swimming is apparent, not every device or piece of equipment is needed by every swimmer. You should select what is appropriate and useful for your particular technique problems, training level, and workout routine. In addition, keep in mind that one important reason to use any training equipment is injury prevention. Anyone who is susceptible to injury or has had an injury should work extra hard with training devices to build up that anatomical part to prevent further damage.

No matter what the stage of or reason for training, all swimmers should progress gradually when using training equipment, moving up in weights or repetitions only as specific levels are mastered. It is also important to have coaches or trainers demonstrate new or unfamiliar exercise devices and then follow up to make sure the athlete is performing all exercises correctly. Only then can the greatest benefits in the minimum amount of time be realized.

In-Water Gear

Caps. Many swimmers wear rubber swim caps to protect their hair from heavy chemical concentrations in pool water, as well as to keep hair out of their eyes. Some swimmers also say that swim caps streamline their progress in the water. For ultradistance swimming, a rubber cap helps preserve body heat (the head loses heat faster than any other part of the body) and gives the swimmer a little more energy for the long event.

Earplugs. For swimmers who experience repeated ear infections or inner-ear discomfort, earplugs are essential. Made of soft pliable rubber, they are easy to insert and remove. For fit and comfort, some swimmers may need custom-molded earplugs. If regular earplugs continually fall out, or if a swimmer has persistent ear infections, a physician should be consulted for specialized equipment.

Fins. Fins for swimmers in training evolved from those developed for scuba divers. Like scuba fins, training fins are made of rubber, but are somewhat smaller and lighter. Used for propulsion purposes, fins give a swimmer a feeling of being lifted and pushed forward more rapidly than in normal swimming. The swimmer's legs are held higher in the water, and his or her body rides more smoothly and comfortably in the water. The sensations of speed and flowing are not, however, the main purpose for using fins. Rather, it is to help swimmers practice kicking and to work on perfecting strokes.

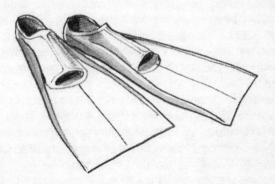

Fins

Goggles. Swimmers often experience eye discomfort from chemicals in pool water. Goggles designed especially for swimming can help prevent redness and watering eyes. The best goggle frames are made of rubber with a synthetic foam surrounding the lens orbits to seal out water. Lenses come in different colors, with darker shades for outdoor swimming and lighter shades for indoor use. While goggles may be desirable for many swimmers, it is best not to spend more than $5 to $10 on them and to buy

Goggles

replacements when the frames start to deteriorate or water seeps in. More expensive antifog goggles have come on the market recently. If fogging is a serious and continuous problem, this high-tech version might be worth the investment.

Hand paddles. As an aid in practicing specific strokes, as well as getting additional and continuous resistance, hand paddles are a technological breakthrough. Made of hard plastic, hand paddles are somewhat larger than normal hands and are attached to the wrists and palms with rubber tubing. They come in various sizes and shapes, but also can be custom designed so that the swimmer catches and pulls the water properly through the entire phase of the stroke.

Kickboards. It is imperative to have a kickboard in order to concentrate on kicking motions without worrying about keeping the upper body afloat. Used by beginners and advanced swimmers alike, this piece of equipment allows swimmers to practice almost every kicking motion in isolation. Constructed of Styrofoam, kickboards are rectangular with a rounded nose and weigh from 6 oz. to 1 pound.

Noseplugs. Swimmers who have sinus problems or who experience any nasal discomfort should use noseplugs. Made of soft rubber, they have a rigid nose piece that adheres to the nose and seals the nostrils.

Pull-buoys. To prevent leg drag while working on stroke technique, swimmers must use pull-buoys. These rounded Styrofoam flotation devices fit between a swimmer's upper thighs to hold them in a lifted position. This permits the swimmer to practice strokes without the feeling of continuous downpull on the legs.

Swimsuits. Today's speediest suits are made of nylon or Lycra and are skin-tight to provide swimmers with the most streamlined shape to propel them through the water. Lycra allows water to pass through without catching in pockets next to the skin. The growing popularity of triathalons and other open-water long-distance events has created a demand for swimsuits that conserve body heat. Lightweight neoprene rubber vests and body suits have been used, but lighter synthetic materials are being tested for greater comfort and mobility.

Swim tunes. Although practicing specific strokes and kicks requires concentration, it is the repetition of swimming strokes that is fundamental to achieving efficiency. This can be borrrrring! Music is the best way to relieve the tedium, which is why, in years past, swim teams had music piped underwater while they practiced. Today, the individual swimmer can use a waterproof radio–cassette player while practicing laps or training for ultra-distance in pools or during open-water workouts. *Caution:* this is not to be confused with a Sony Walkman, which is not for underwater use.

Tethered swim devices. These devices permit swimmers to practice in place, doing different strokes at varying intensities without having to think of staying afloat. A flotation harness is belted to the swimmer's waist, maintaining his or her body in a functional swimming position. A tethering cord is attached to the side of the pool, anchored to the bottom of the pool, or hooked to some piece of equipment on the deck. With the device around the waist, the swimmer is suspended comfortably to practice.

Timers. Friends and coaches can help by timing laps with a stopwatch, but for solitary workouts most pools have large sweep-hand clocks. If a pool doesn't have a timing clock, a waterproof watch can be worn during practice sessions. The most useful types display total lap times, splits, and other aspects of swimming practice as well as overall time for ultradistance swimming sessions. Split times can be recorded throughout a workout session. For example, swimming 400 meters, a split can be recorded at the end of each 100. In addition to timing laps, swimmers can also monitor their heart rate with a waterproof watch that has a special readout for this purpose.

Dryland Training Gear

There are many simple items that can make a swimmer's life more comfortable and his or her training more effective, but often they are overlooked in preparing for workouts. These range from warm-up suits to a notebook for recording workout sessions.

It is, however, the modern training equipment used by athletes in any number of sports that is the most revolutionary and useful breakthrough for improving results. Some of this equipment, such as free weights, has been around for many years, but sports trainers have only recently devised ways to significantly boost training effectiveness through its use. Resistance machines, pulleys, and small, lightweight devices that can travel with an athlete are also significant equipment that every athlete should know about.

Not every type of workout equipment is available at every fitness center, nor is every training device suited for every swimmer. You need to shop around for the right kind of fitness center that is staffed with knowledgeable, experienced trainers who can guide you in using the equipment. After you are shown how to use a machine or lift a weight, be sure to continue to work the equipment as it was demonstrated. Only with correct use can you realize the maximum benefits from training devices.

In addition to a competent training staff, a good fitness center should offer nutrition and cardiovascular evaluations. It should be reasonably convenient so that long travel time will not be necessary and should have a wide range of operating hours. Basic equipment for a good fitness center includes free weights, machine weights, stationary bikes, rowing machines, and other specialized equipment for swimmers.

Keep in mind that you don't necessarily need to join a fitness center to do dryland workouts. Home fitness equipment often achieves the training goal and is much less expensive to use.

Apparel. Getting to and from the swim area and even hanging around before or after meets requires specialized clothing. Robes or warm-up suits are needed to keep warm or, in the case of warm-up and sweat suits, to do flexibility exercises and other dryland workouts. For footwear, you will need sandles or clogs that do not collect water, and for indoor training you should have rubber-soled sports shoes. Naturally, you should have a good-sized travel bag to tote all this gear, including towels and personal cosmetics.

Biokinetic swim bench. This is one of the few machines on which a swimmer can simulate actual stroke technique through

Swim bench

resistance pull patterns without getting wet. This device is not often found at fitness centers, but it is often available at colleges or major swim clubs. It can be an important training tool for advanced swimmers.

Free weights. Popularly known as barbells and dumbbells, free weights provide an athlete the opportunity to do many exercises through a full range of motion. Fitness centers almost always have free weights, but they can be purchased for home use for about $40 to $50. One advantage of fitness centers is the availability of benches on which the angles of resistance can be changed. This varies the sites of tension, helping to build different muscle groups. It is a good idea to buy a lifting belt to protect the lower back from strain when lifting very heavy weights. Lifting gloves may be desirable to protect the hands.

Barbells are steel bars 5 to 7 feet in length that hold plates of various weights at each end. Barbells are usually stored on lifting racks from which the user lifts them. To keep the weights from slipping off the ends, end caps or collars should be attached and screwed tight at both ends of the bar.

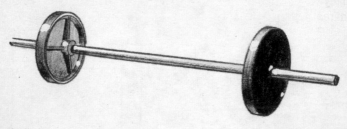

Barbells

Dumbbells are smaller, lighter versions of barbells. They may be used individually to exercise a single arm or both arms in unison.

Dumbbells

Machines. Various weight-training machines have come into popular use in recent years. Unlike barbells and dumbbells, most of these machines permit movement in a very limited range, thus exercising specific muscles. This has the advantage of developing selected muscles and, when following the prescribed repetition patterns, of causing fewer accidental strains and weight overloads.

Air-resistance machines use compressed air to regulate the amount of resistance for an exercise. The user dials the amount of compressed air he or she wishes on a gauge and then works for a specific amount of time on the selected machine.

Cable machines use a cable and pulley system to lift a stack of weights. These machines permit a wider range of motion than many of the modern exercise machines, but they are still more limited than free weights.

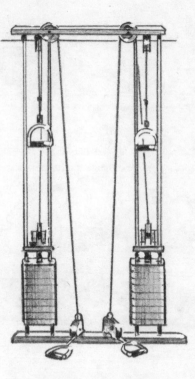

Cable machine

Cam-activated machines are able to maintain a fairly constant resistance throughout an exercise movement, because a cam keeps tension on the weights. A cable or chain holding stacks of weights is grooved into the cam.

Hydraulic machines have liquid-filled shock absorbers connected to a system of levers to change resistance. These machines permit a smooth motion throughout a full range of movement.

S.P.O.R.T. Cord. This device is made of lightweight, durable surgical tubing that has handgrips attached to both ends. It also comes with an adjustable belt, a webbed nylon strap to hold the tubing in a doorjamb, and nylon foot stirrups. When rolled up, everything fits easily into a small nylon bag for storage or to carry on the road for exercising when away from home. The device can provide resistance while duplicating many swim strokes. The S.P.O.R.T. Cord is used by many recreational and professional athletes.

S.P.O.R.T. Cord

Training diary. Keeping a record of what you do during each training session not only lets you know how you are progressing, but provides inspiration and direction during periods when you are at a plateau and don't seem to be improving. Just looking back over notes and reviewing progress can buoy your spirits for more work. Write down what you want to accomplish in each session: warm-up exercises; flexibility stretches; strength training sets, repetitions and amount of weight; aerobic or anaerobic training with time, sets, and repetitions; and cool-down exercises. Entries should be brief but consistent. Many swimmers also include their heart rate and body weight and make note of any injuries suffered in training or competition.

When using any training equipment, it is very important to set a realistic schedule of workouts and expected progress. Goals set too high lead to discouragement; set too low, they produce little improvement. A fitness trainer can help you set these goals and can monitor your progress, but each athlete must track his or her training schedule. A notebook or diary is a good aid, but only in your head and heart can you truthfully know how well you are doing.

CHAPTER 3

WARM-UP/COOL-DOWN TRAINING

The necessity for warming up before an exercise, training session, or competition and cooling down after such exertion is understood by most experienced and inexperienced athletes. At the same time, this necessity is often forgotten, overlooked, or just plain ignored. Most people are so eager to get on with their exercise and get it over with that they skip the essential warm-up and cool-down segments of their training regimen.

Because flexibility, the basic beneficial component of warming up and cooling down, is fundamental to later performance and exertion, the importance of warm-ups and cool-downs cannot be overstressed. Flexibility results in freer movement about joint areas that involve muscles, tendons, ligaments, and soft connective tissue. These anatomical parts form working relationships that permit more or less motion to occur at the joints. Swimmers in particular are often lax about doing flexibility exercises, because swimming is a low-impact sport in which the level of joint stress at the knee and hip is nonmeasurable. For this reason, many swimmers believe they don't need warming up and cooling down—that the sport itself is adequate to give them plenty of flexibility.

In the final analysis, every individual has his or her own flexibility patterns and limitations resulting from anatomical differences, activity levels while growing up, selection of sports, and age. Some people are inherently stiff or may not have developed flexibility in formative years; some sports, other than swimming, do not encourage development of flexibility patterns. In addition, people tend to lose flexibility as they age. A program of consistent and sound flexibility exercises can, however, alleviate all of these limitations to a greater or lesser extent. **The range of motion can be increased, even as we grow older.**

Flexibility Benefits

Understanding what flexibility does should help you follow a disciplined program in doing warm-up and cool-down exercises. Certainly, such a program can prepare you for swimming, but it also can reduce the chances of injury and muscle soreness from exertion. Some swimmers use the flexibility-exercise time to mentally rehearse stroke patterns or to review training sequences and race strategy. In addition, such exercises physiologically stimulate metabolic functions, and after a swimming workout or competition they help the body return to its normal metabolic homeostasis or equilibrium.

Scientifically, a warm-up session should be directed toward gradually increasing body-core (inner body) temperature. This allows for easier delivery of oxygen to muscles, permitting them to work at a smooth, fluid tempo and ultimately producing an improvement in the mechanical efficiency of the joints. At the same time, warming up allows nerve impulses to travel more rapidly through the body and increases the sensitivity of nerve receptors. This in turn assists the central nervous system and the muscles in executing correct and efficient flexibility exercises in preparation for a sports activity. It also protects the body from injury.

In addition to an increase in oxygen to the muscles, blood flow is increased to muscles. This increased amount of blood not only delivers more oxygen to the working muscles, but carries more nutrients that are important for peak metabolic functioning.

In contrast, the cool-down phase of an exercise session attempts to slow the metabolic processes of the body. Gradually the heart rate, blood flow, and body temperature decrease through the easing off of activity. In addition, lactic acid—a metabolic by-product of exercise found in muscles—can be eliminated and resynthesized to provide additional energy. This is particularly important when an exercise or activity has been very intense, causing lactic acid to build up in muscle cells. Once the lactic acid reaches a level that the muscles cannot tolerate, the metabolic functions begin to shut down and the athlete finds that he or she cannot continue the activity. This condition can occur during high-intensity workouts, such as intervals or sprints, or it may occur at the end of a 200-meter freestyle. A combination of active and static cool-down exercises can assist in eliminating built-up lactic acid so that the athlete can return to a normal level of functioning for other activities.

In short, the purposes of warming up are to increase optimal performance and to prevent injury. Cooling down allows the human machine to unwind slowly without stress to any of its parts.

It is easy to understand the value of the warm-up and cool-down phases of exercise or competition, but for the impatient athlete it may still seem to take too much time. Recreational swimmers can use the warm-up time to mentally rehearse strokes and technique. However, this mental process does not replace the actual warm-up phase.

In a number of sports, team coaches make valuable use of warm-up time by having athletes prepare for an upcoming event with mental rehearsals of what they will do in competition. Before the event, spectators often see athletes going through the motions of warming up with faraway expressions on their faces. Their concentration seems to be channeled well beyond the movements of their bodies; clearly, their thoughts are directed elsewhere.

It is impossible to know the precise value of such intense concentration while warming up prior to an event, but the winners and champions are often seen cooling down with the same intensity, although their faces may have more animated expressions. We do know, however, that dedicating as much as 15 to 20 minutes to warming up and cooling down has concrete payoffs for such athletes. They take the trophies home.

Warm-up and Cool-down Methods

Obviously, muscles can be warmed from external (passive) sources such as hot showers, whirlpool baths, massages, heating pads, and other types of therapy. Such actions get oxygen and blood flowing to the muscles and joints and may be useful when an athlete has experienced an injury.

Far more effective, however, are active warm-up exercises. These may be either of two types: a dryland flexibility program or specific exercises that closely duplicate swimming motions. Both types of active warm-up exercises increase muscle temperature more rapidly and more effectively than passive warm-ups.

Flexibility programs can incorporate stretching that is static, that moves, or that involves proprioceptor neuromuscular facilitation (PNF). Static stretching is slow, deliberate movement until an end point is reached when muscles will not tolerate any additional pull because further stretching would be painful. When the end point is reached, the position is held. Movement stretching involves motion at specific joints through a broad range of motion, such as doing a waist twist with a slow and deliberate movement. PNF stretching utilizes specific receptors in joints and muscles to facilitate nerve transmission so that there is no injury to the muscle or joint involved. This stretching is performed with a partner.

The types of warm-up exercises that duplicate swimming motions are often done with in-water aids such as kickboards or pull-buoys. Or they might simply be leisurely practice sessions that include strokes, kicks, or starts and turns. These sport-specific warm-up exercises not only engage the muscle groups that will be used later in practice or competition, but they activate the neuromuscular system, making the muscles more quickly responsive to an aroused neural input. In other words, the entire central nervous system is preparing itself for the workout session or race.

Cool-down sessions can include either or both types of exercise, but in reverse order. A swimmer gradually reduces swimming speed and intensity and lets movements become more leisurely. Once out of the pool, stretching eases off to gentle pulls.

Why stretching works to warm up or cool down the body is one of the marvels of human anatomy. Receptors located throughout the body transmit to the central nervous system messages telling the body what is going on at any particular time. When a person is stretching, the muscle spindle receptors located in the muscle sense changes in muscle length and institute a stretch reflex in which the spindles are activated to protect the muscle so that it does not overstretch. The stretch reflex goes something like this: 1) muscle begins stretching; 2) nerves send impulses from receptors to spinal cord; 3) impulses move from spinal cord back to stretched muscle; 4) muscle contracts to resist further stretching. Without this mechanism, a dynamic stretch or movement could cause injury to the muscle.

The golgi tendon receptors (located in tendons near the muscle being stretched) also respond to the tension of a stretching situation, causing the stretching muscle to relax and thus providing another protection from overstretching. For example, if you do a seated hamstring stretch and hold the position for 10 to 15 seconds, the golgi tendon receptors may sense too much tension and direct the hamstring muscles to relax.

PNF stretching utilizes the stretch reflex mechanism so that contraction and relaxation of alternating muscle groups occur. This produces a facilitated stretch in which activated nerve impulses are received by the central nervous system and sent to the muscles, which promotes an efficient, protective stretch.

Movement stretching must be preceded by some type of warm-up, because during this type of stretching, muscle spindles, which respond to changes in muscle length, are being stretched at a rapid rate. It is so fast, in fact, that the golgi tendon receptors do not have time to fire. Movement stretching can be included in swimming warm-ups.

Every workout session should include stretching exercises to work muscles at the neck, shoulders, hips, knees, and ankles. Swimmers may want to work especially hard on specific stretches that increase the range of motion for stroke length at the catch and pull phases of the stroke. This is one area where tangible results from a flexibility program can be seen.

When and Where to Stretch

How much warming up and cooling down is necessary for each individual varies, but generally 15 to 20 minutes before and after a workout or a competition is recommended. The regimen can be tailored to the individual but should not be so vigorous or intense that it causes fatigue that can inhibit athletic performance. In addition, some authorities suggest that no more than 15 minutes should lapse between the warm-up and the start of an event. Too much time may allow the body to cool down to a near-normal state.

A typical warm-up session should include stretching, stroke and kick patterns, and psychological awareness—all of which build in intensity through the session. Such a warm-up session might look like this:

Poolside. Walking, easy stretches, and loosening.

In water. Leisurely freestyle swimming for 50 to 100 yards is appropriate for recreational swimmers, but advanced swimmers may want to do as much as 100 to 200 yards, increasing intensity for the final 50 yards. Recreational swimmers may want to do other strokes for another 50 to 100 yards, ending the warm-up with 50 yards of kicking drills. Advanced swimmers can practice additional strokes for 200 yards, followed by 50 to 100 yards of kicking drills and ending with 5 to 10 (each) turns and starts.

Poolside. Stretching exercises with or without a partner.

While all of these exercises can be altered to suit individual needs and events, the results should increase heart rate, particularly during the swimming warm-up, and elevate body core temperature.

Cool-down sessions might duplicate the warm-ups, but going in the other direction. Following a heavy workout session, it may be necessary to simply swim in the lane for 5 minutes and then do a series of stretches on the pool deck. The ultimate aim, however, is accomplished: to reduce heart rate to 100 to 110 beats per minute or lower.

In workouts it is important to vary warm-ups and cool-downs, not only to work all parts of the body but to avoid burn-out. Incorporate two or three stretching exercises from each category described in the following pages.

Most important, do it! Warming up and cooling down are as important as the events or workouts themselves.

What and How to Exercise

There are numerous stretching exercises that provide variety of movement and yet include all the essential parts of the body. Each swimmer must structure his or her regimen according to individual objectives and physical ability. It is important, however, for anyone who has had a history of spinal or joint problems to consult a physician before embarking on an intense flexibility program.

For all of the exercises described here, the body should be kept as comfortable as possible without excessive strain and using a soft surface or mat for those that are done in a prone position. **It is important to emphasize very slow movements to reach the hold positions for stretches, but to avoid extreme positions that place stress on joints.** Stretching sessions should be progressive, moving from static to PNF and then to movement stretching that involves a full range of motion in the joints.

In a flexibility program that emphasizes primary swimming muscles, the question is how far to stretch. The answer is an individual matter, but stretch to a point where tightness or tension is felt in muscles, not beyond. Avoid pain, at all costs. In a correct stretch, the muscles and soft tissues have a feeling of being pulled, but there is no feeling of dynamic, strong contractions. As more stretching is done, a gradual sense of the correct amount of stretch is realized.

Many athletes overlook correct breathing during stretching exercises. It is important to relax and exhale from the lungs as positions are approached and held during static or PNF stretches. Doing this consciously may even improve the range of motion— particularly in those stretches that seem difficult or uncomfortable.

Static Stretching

Neck. Stretch your neck four ways. First, move your chin toward your chest and hold this position for 10 to 15 seconds. Second, move your right ear toward your right shoulder and hold for 10 to 15 seconds. Third, look toward the sky or ceiling and hold for 10 to 15 seconds. Fourth, move your left ear toward your left shoulder and hold for 10 to 15 seconds.

Shoulders (deltoid muscles). While holding a towel, bring your left hand to the base of your neck, keeping your left elbow raised. Use your right hand behind your back to grip the other end of the towel and provide downward resistance. Hold this stretched position for 10 to 15 seconds and repeat the position 5 times for each shoulder.

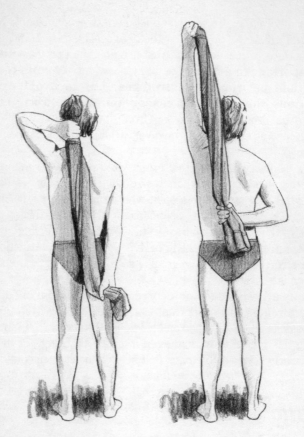

Towel shoulder stretch

Back (latissimus dorsi muscles). Start this stretch from a position resting on your hands and knees with your palms flat on the floor. Slowly sit back on your lower legs, keeping your palms in the original position. Concentrate on pulling back with your back muscles while keeping your hands in the original starting position. Hold the lowered position for 10 to 15 seconds and repeat the exercise 5 times.

Back

Back of thighs (hamstring muscles). From a seated position with your legs straight, slowly bend at the waist, lowering your head toward your knees. Let your hands move along the outsides of your legs in the direction of your ankles. While stretching into this lowered position, slowly breathe out. Hold the position for 10 to 15 seconds and repeat the exercise 5 times.

Front of thighs (quadriceps muscles). From a standing position, place your left hand on a bleacher or chair for balance and allow your left leg to bend slightly to aid balance. Bend your right leg back toward your buttocks and grasp your right foot with your right hand. Apply a steady resistance by pulling the foot toward your buttocks. Hold the position for 10 seconds and repeat 5 times with each leg.

Back of calves (gastrocnemius muscles and Achilles tendon). Stand about 3 feet away from a wall as you face it. Rest your hands and forehead on the wall as you bend one knee and bring that knee and foot toward the wall. Keep your other leg back and hold it straight with your heel flat on the floor. Slowly push your hips and front knee toward the wall until you feel a strong stretch on the muscles and tendons in the back of the straightened leg. Hold this position for 10 seconds and repeat the stretch 5 times for each leg.

PNF Stretching

Back of thighs and lower back. While seated with legs straight, slowly bend at the waist, lowering your head toward your knees as your hands move along the sides of your legs. Have a partner apply a steady but light pressure on your shoulder blades until you

Back of thighs and lower back

reach your lowest position at the bottom of the stretch. Hold this position for 10 seconds. As you return to an upright position, have your partner continue to provide a strong, steady resistance on your shoulders. Repeat the exercise 5 times.

Groin and lower back. In a seated position on the floor, spread your legs into a large "V" position, keeping them straight. Place both palms flat on the floor between your legs and slowly bend at the waist while lowering your head and sliding your hands forward. Have your partner apply slow, steady pressure against your shoulder blades as you slowly exhale and reach the stretched position. Hold this bottom position for 5 to 10 seconds. Repeat the entire exercise 5 times.

Front of thighs and hip flexors. (This exercise can be performed with or without a partner.) While standing on one slightly flexed leg, use one hand for balance by holding on to a chair or bleacher. Reach down with the other hand and grasp the top of the opposite foot/ankle joint and slowly pull it back toward your buttocks. During every 3 to 6 inches of movement, stop and hold your ankle firmly as you resist (isometrically) as strongly as possible by pushing the foot forward for about 5 seconds. Do 3 resistance stops for each leg. If you have a partner, have him or her kneel near the leg that is being exercised and grasp the top of the foot/ankle joint with both hands. At the resistance stops, the partner prevents forward motion. Repeat each leg 3 to 5 times.

Shoulders. While standing, extend your arms backward as far as possible without bending at the elbows. Have a partner grasp

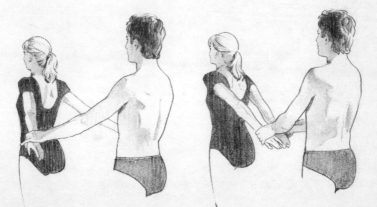

Partner shoulder stretch

your wrists with a very light pressure and slowly stretch your shoulders and arms by crossing your arms. It is very important that your partner realize the need for being very gentle to avoid injury to your shoulders. Hold the stretched position for 10 seconds and repeat the exercise 5 times.

Back of calves. While you are seated on the floor with both legs straight and feet pointing at a 90-degree angle, have a partner cup the heel of one foot in one hand as he or she uses the other hand to provide resistance at the ball of the foot. Your partner will need to be in a kneeling or seated position in front of you. The first part of this exercise is pressing your foot against a partner's hand as he or she resists this movement. Hold this position for 5 seconds. The second part of the exercise comes after a brief relaxation of your foot and ankle. Have your partner press your ankle toward your shin to provide stretching for your calf and heel cord. Hold this stretched position for 5 seconds and repeat the entire exercise 5 times for each ankle.

Movement Stretches

Back of thighs and groin. In a side lunge position, slowly lower your torso to the floor as far as possible. Try to keep your inside foot flat on the floor and use the heel of your outside foot for

Back of thighs and groin

balance. Use a slow, smooth motion to position yourself into the stretch, and alternate from side to side. In the lowered position, stretch for 2 to 3 seconds and then rise and move to the opposite side. Repeat this stretch 5 times for each side.

Back of thighs and buttocks. In a stride position with your front leg bent and your back leg straight, slowly do a front kick with your back leg. The first few kicks should be very slow and low, but you can gradually increase the speed and height of your kicks. Repeat this exercise 10 times for each leg.

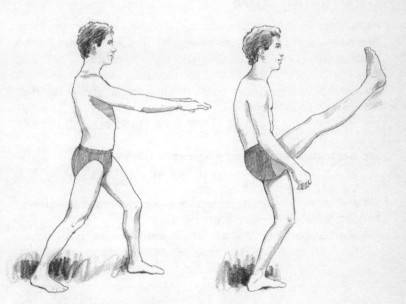

Back of thighs and buttocks

Shoulders, lower back, and waist. While sitting on a chair or bench, place a long pole or broom handle behind your neck, grasping both ends with your hands as far apart as is comfortable. Using the pole for leverage, slowly rotate your shoulders and waist in one direction and then in the other, keeping the pole handle parallel to the floor. Keep your shoulders level and your head facing directly ahead throughout this exercise. Repeat this stretch 25 times in each direction.

Middle and lower back. This exercise can be performed in the shallow end of a pool or on the pool deck where there is a bleacher or railing. While standing, extend both arms straight, keeping them roughly parallel to the pool bottom or floor. Grasp the ledge of the pool or top of the bleacher with your palms flat and, using just your fingertips for balance, slowly bend your knees to lower your body into a half-squat position. Hold this position for 5 seconds. Repeat the exercise 10 times.

Stretching Tips

There are several important points to remember while doing these exercises:

- Stretch to a maximum position, but avoid bouncing movement once in the position.
- It is essential to exhale slowly during the stretching phase of an exercise.
- Exercises should be done in a prescribed order, beginning with static stretches, then doing PNF stretches, and finishing with movement stretches.
- Perform all stretching exercises in a slow, controlled manner, avoiding quick or bouncing motions.
- Most important, be sure to *do* warm-up and cool-down flexibility exercises. They can be vital to your improvement.

CHAPTER 4

BUILDING MUSCLES

In the last decade, resistance training, or muscle building as it is popularly known, has become increasingly important to people who are serious participants in sports, both at recreational and

competitive levels. Almost all athletes realize that muscle development is vital to improvement, so they include weight training programs in their workouts.

But being strong is more than simply having well-developed muscles or being able to lift heavy weights. There are actually three separate functions involved in muscle development. There is muscular strength, which is the physiological basis for all the other muscular functions. There is muscular power, which is explosiveness and speed of movement. And there is muscular endurance, which enables an athlete to sustain repeated muscular work.

These three functions, although sometimes separate in application and use in sports, are interdependent and overlap in muscular endeavors. But in most sports it is important to concentrate on one or two muscular functions. In swimming, the major training emphasis should be on power, particularly during the preseason and in-season sessions. The continuous stroke and kicking motions in swimming require well-developed muscular power to produce efficient technique and speed.

Strength in all its forms gives an athlete a competitive edge. But strength must be acquired—you don't "play" yourself into shape or swim yourself into muscular fitness—through the hard work of resistance training.

The term *pumping iron* is usually associated with body builders, men and women who do weight training to sculpt and shape their bodies to be judged in competition. Weight lifting is another aspect of pumping iron and is often associated with Olympic competitions in which very strong and quick athletes use explosive motions to hoist heavy barbells above their heads, hold that position for a brief period, and then let the weight come down with a resounding crash and a grunt.

These are not, however, the body images that swimmers aim for through resistance training. Swimmers want long, supple muscles, not the bulges of the power lifter or the body sculptor. Muscle development, using an athlete's own body weight, free weights, weight machines, pulley systems, elastic resistance devices, and sport-specific devices, which duplicate the movements of a particular sport, can give a swimmer precisely the kind of shape he or she wants to have.

Besides the sheer increase in muscle size and capacity for work, weight training also provides injury-prevention benefits. Swimming is a sport requiring repetitions of strokes and kicks in which muscle groups are constantly being asked to contract, relax, and contract again. This places extreme anatomical demands on body joints, where muscles act as bridgework over and around the joints. Just as a bridge must function as a unit with a sound structure from end to end, so the muscular structure surrounding each joint in the body requires integrity for efficient, maximum performance. For an athlete, this integrity comes from an increase in muscular strength, power, and endurance, in addition to inherently sound connective tissue, tendons, and ligaments. The end result can help minimize injuries resulting from the athlete's principal sport, as well as from training situations.

Muscle Make-up

Competitive swimming consists of sprint-type events from 50 to 200 meters and distance events that go up to 1,500 meters in conventional competition, but as much as 1½ to 2 miles in ultradistance events. Whether a swimmer wants to compete or merely to enjoy the rewards of efficient swimming for his own sake, workout requirements can be chosen selectively by training for either sprint or distance or combining the two disciplines to achieve a rounded program.

The bottom line is to train according to individual demands and make-up. An athlete needs to understand his or her requirements and then create a training regimen to meet them. To select events in which one can most easily excel—or at least to understand when and why an athlete seems superior in one event over another—it is necessary to understand how muscles differ.

Skeletal muscle, which is the contracting force for all human movement, is made up of two types of fiber: one is a slow-twitching type, the other is fast-twitching. The relative speed of the twitches is determined by the cellular properties and physiological characteristics of the fibers.

Slow-twitch muscle fibers have a high aerobic capacity that makes them very efficient in using oxygen carried in the bloodstream to a dense capillary network that leads to more capillaries in the working muscles. This efficiency allows an athlete to perform a sport for an extended period of time without undue fatigue, as long as the muscles receive an adequate supply of oxygen.

Fast-twitch muscle fibers, on the other hand, do not require efficient utilization of oxygen, but rather use stored energy and glycogen that is derived from carbohydrates. *An*aerobic means without oxygen and refers to the short periods of time when an athlete's muscles are operating during sprints or intense, fast action. The fast-twitch fibers permit muscles to contract rapidly and with great power, but only for brief periods of time before they become fatigued.

While an average person has approximately a 50:50 ratio of fast- and slow-twitch fibers, some elite athletes have a preponderance of one or the other type of fiber in

their muscles. Moreover, the distribution of fiber types varies in different muscle groups, due to genetic inheritance. It is the combination of the predominant fiber type plus the location of the fibers that often determines the sport and the particular event an athlete selects.

Muscle biopsies, in which samples of fiber are examined microscopically to determine cellular properties, have contributed significantly to understanding the physiological make-up of sprint versus endurance athletes. For example, in running, sprinters usually have a greater number of fast-twitch fibers, while marathon runners average 70 to 80 percent slow-twitch fibers.

Training does, however, play a major role in enhancing muscle tissue for optimal performance. Aerobic workouts—long periods of continuous swimming—develop aerobic properties in slow-twitch fibers, while anaerobic workouts—a series of fast and intense short sprints—develop anaerobic properties in fast-twitch fibers. What is significant is that swimmers, no matter what their particular event, need portions of both types of workout to contribute to their fiber types. In competition, the swimmer's body places emphasis on one type of muscle fiber over the other, depending on the intensity and duration of the event. In a sprint event, the predominant muscles used are the fast-twitch type, while in a distance event the body calls upon the slow-twitch muscles for maximum output. In middle-distance events, both fiber types work equally hard. The selection of one fiber type over another is called a recruitment pattern and seems to occur as instinctively as individual athletes select swimming events that work best for their physical and mental make-ups.

For many young or inexperienced swimmers, deciding between the two types of swimming—the sprint or the endurance event—is difficult and sometimes prevents them from concentrating on a training program that will provide the greatest benefits. **Each person is born with a set fiber composition that cannot be altered or changed, although one type can be developed more than the other type through training.** To find the most ideal personal performance events, an athlete needs to analyze past and present swim workout preferences, review competition results and times, ask knowledgeable and impartial coaches for advice, and honestly assess inner drives and needs.

When the selection is made, working to full potential is the next goal. Reaching this goal begins with a sound and consistent training program.

Muscle Movement

The first step in developing an effective training regimen is to understand what muscles are doing during swimming motions, both in dryland training and in pool workouts and practice. Only then can an athlete use his or her own body weight, exercise machines, free weights, and elastic resistance devices to the utmost in training.

The fundamental movement of muscles in sports is contraction, which occurs in four different and distinct ways.

Isometric contractions are static, rather than dynamic or movement oriented. One example of an isotonic contraction is placing the hands in a "prayer" position and then pressing them together as hard as possible. There is no limb movement, although the muscles are working. Because of this lack of movement, isometric contractions are not highly valuable to athletes and are not often used in strength training for sports.

Isotonic or concentric contractions are dynamic, causing a shortening of muscles through a range of motion. An example would be to lift a jar of jam from a kitchen counter and place it on a shelf overhead. The triceps on the backs of the upper arms would be used as the arms are extended. The weakness of isotonic contractions is that the muscles are under different amounts of tension as the limbs move through the exercise. At various points and at different angles, the muscles involved are using more or less tension, rather than maintaining equal tension throughout the movement. What is happening is that the angle of pull on the muscles is constantly changing, making the muscles work harder or easier at some angles than at others.

Eccentric or negative contractions are often used in conjunction with isotonic contractions. Eccentric contractions lengthen the muscles while they are under tension. Thus, while the triceps shorten in putting the jam jar on a high shelf (performing an isotonic contraction), returning the jam to the kitchen counter lengthens the muscles, and as long as they remain under tension, muscles get beneficial development. An important principle concerning eccentric contractions is that they should be performed more slowly than isotonic contractions. Only then can an athlete realize the balanced training from the combination of isotonic and eccentric exercises.

Isokinetic contractions are the byproducts of modern technology in exercise equipment. Throughout an exercise motion, tension is maintained at the maximum force, and the speed of movement is kept constant so that the limb or body part cannot move any faster than a preselected setting allows. Such contractions, of course, can be performed only on sophisticated exercise equipment such as the Cybex or Lido devices. The advantages of isokinetic contractions are that the muscles are forced to adapt to the speed set on the machine, and the machine creates a maximum force throughout a full range of motion. An athlete can concentrate on slow, medium, or fast speeds, depending on what he or she needs for efficient training.

Swimming itself simulates isokinetic exercise, because water creates a similar kind of constant tension and speed resistance to that which machines provide. In training, therefore, swimmers can derive particular benefits from dryland programs with some isokinetic machines, but they should not concentrate solely on such exercises, forgoing other valuable dryland training workouts involving isotonic and eccentric exercises.

Muscle Development

How strong you are, how strong you can be, and even the shape of your muscles depend on several factors. The first and fundamental one is, of course, your inherited characteristics: your body size, limb length, muscle diameter and length, and the make-up of your muscle tissue.

These basic ingredients of a person's anatomy can be enhanced through training to give existing muscles more strength, power, and endurance. Specifically, what resistance training does is increase the size of muscles by increasing the size of the fast- and slow-twitch fibers in the muscles. Within each fiber are myofibrils, which are threadlike and made up of proteins. These myofibrils increase in size and number as more protein is added through the metabolic process of protein synthesis. Muscle hypertrophy (increase in size) is more noticeable in fast-twitch fibers than in slow-twitch fibers, although in some instances there is a gain in strength without a great deal of hypertrophy. Muscles do not continuously increase in size and strength throughout life. Peak development occurs during the early to mid-twenties.

Males have a greater tendency for muscle hypertrophy than females do because of their greater supply of the hormone testosterone. This hormone regulates the size and rate of muscle growth by stimulating protein synthesis. In recent years, however, women athletes have revealed a greater capacity for muscle development than was thought possible just a decade ago. This is not due to greater amounts of testosterone, but to much more vigorous training routines, which have resulted in greater muscle definition and development. **It points up the fact that there is no need for men or women to supplement their diets with testosterone to build muscles.**

In a very subtle way, muscle development is also controlled by the brain and higher portions of the spinal cord. There is some indication from current research that the central nervous system acts as a computer to program movements, which in turn affect the development of muscles.

Training Consequences

Increasing the strength, power, and endurance of muscles through training, or indeed through any kind of hard exertion, often results in muscle soreness. Pain and stiffness may begin as soon as twelve hours after a workout or be delayed as long as five days following exercise. The cause of such soreness has not been precisely identified, but scientific guesstimates are that structural damage to muscle fibers and connective tissue precipitates muscle spasm and pain.

While muscle soreness from exercise is temporary, some athletes find that their muscular force is hindered by pain and their physical performance diminishes as a result. To prevent or minimize such soreness, it is wise to move gradually into untried dryland exercises or increases in the intensity or distance of pool workouts. **Another way to avoid soreness is to allow at**

least 24 to 48 hours to pass between sessions that involve new exercises or increases in workouts.

Studies have shown that caloric expenditures vary from upper- and lower-body exercise routines. In one experiment, male subjects exercised for 36 minutes on machines using standard routines and doing 3 sets of 6 to 9 repetitions with 1-minute rests between each set. For upper-body routines the average energy expenditure was 174 calories per session, while for the lower-body routines the expenditure was 222 calories per session. In similar tests using men and women, it was shown that men expended an average of 170 calories, but women expended only 110 calories in the same time period. These tests were conducted among "normal" subjects who were not doing serious athletic training, so their exercise rate, intensity, duration, and frequency were below that of developing athletes. A swimmer aspiring to high-level recreational or competitive achievements needs to be careful to maintain adequate weight for sustained exertion.

Muscle Functions

The three muscle functions—strength, power, and endurance—overlap in athletic use as well as development. Training to improve any one of these components will result in the improvement of the other two.

The danger is for an athlete to concentrate on a muscle function that is already well developed rather than working toward a balance of functions or emphasizing the one function that is most useful for his or her sport. For instance, there are swimmers who possess excellent strength but are less well developed in their power component—which is the one most needed in their sport. There are other swimmers who have great endurance but lack strength and power. These abilities may come naturally to a particular athlete who then simply continues to work hardest on what seems most comfortable. The proper emphasis should include all three muscle functions, with more emphasis on power just prior to and during the swim season.

Power is essentially work divided by time. The swimmer's aim is to move the resistance as quickly as possible. (In algebraic terms it would be expressed as $\frac{(f \times d)}{t}$, where f is force, d is distance, and t is time.) Because speed is integral to power, it is possible to improve power, not only through muscle training, but by improving motor skills such as timing, reactions, and coordination—all of which are components of speed.

The basic method of building power, however, is through resistance or muscle training. Over a period of time, this results in a physiological increase in force production during slow contractions as well as speedier contractions.

Swimmers are especially concerned with having explosive power that produces a highly active, useful movement, but with neuromuscular control. To do this, it is best to do some training with lighter resistance (less weight) and more repetitions.

There is a point, however, just before a competition, when it may be beneficial to taper off power training. According to a recent study, college swimmers who had been swimming an average of 9,500 yards per day began cutting back on their yardage about two weeks before a major race. They were down to 3,500 yards per day just before the event, but their arm power as measured on a hi-tech swim bench had increased significantly. It was hypothesized that the gradual reduction in training allowed their muscles to gain tension development because of muscle-contracting mechanisms and influences of the nervous system, which may in turn have increased their power output.

Tests like these have led many swimmers to taper off training from five days to two weeks before a major competition. More research is needed to verify such tapering-off programs, and each swimmer must approach new concepts like these on an individual basis. They work for some people some of the time, but not all people all of the time.

While putting an emphasis on muscle power training, swimmers should not overlook training in the other two muscle functions, strength and endurance.

Strength can be defined as the maximum amount of weight lifted in one repetition or the greatest amount of force generated during a maximum contraction. It is similar to a law of physics that defines work, where force times distance ($f \times d$) is the foundation for functional motion. It is easy to see why strength is the foundation of any muscle-training program, for without an adequate strength base it is difficult to develop power and endurance.

Strength training emphasizes the amount of resistance that an athlete can move through a prescribed distance. Done on machines, with free weights or with elastic resistance devices, the force developed is a result of muscles contracting and producing tension, which lifts the resistance or weight.

The final muscle function, endurance, can be described as repeated muscle contractions over a period of time. Some muscular endurance is needed for all swimming events, although sprints use less than middle-distance or long-distance events. For this reason, muscular endurance training should be interwoven into all workout programs. Often endurance can be combined with power training so that each function benefits. Endurance should not, however, be viewed as an end in itself, but rather a continuous—ideally year-round—training regimen that provides variety as well as physiological gains for an athlete.

In the final analysis, though, the foundation of a good training program is increased muscle strength, power, and endurance. This kind of muscle development provides physiological gains as well as aids in preventing injuries. Modern resistance-training equipment and techniques have helped to make athletes stronger and quicker and have enabled them to maintain these qualities throughout each training session.

CHAPTER 5

RESISTANCE TRAINING
TECHNIQUES

Swimming is unquestionably one of the best activities for total body conditioning, because it involves most of the major muscle groups as well as the cardiovascular system. Through swimming you can build muscles and develop your cardiovascular system, but if you want to get there fast—increase the power of strokes and improve lap times—a resistance-training program is essential.

Successful college and Olympic swimmers know this, and they spend a great deal of time doing resistance training outside the water. They have developed programs using specialized and sophisticated equipment as well as conventional devices to help increase their total body fitness.

Although the goal of this aspect of the training program is to improve muscle strength, power, and endurance, resistance exercises should be selected to simulate swimming motions. This will specifically develop those muscles most valuable for swimming.

The Training Process

The basis for all muscle development is progressive overload in which resistance is gradually added. Once a certain weight has been consistently lifted, pulled, or pushed within the workout requirements, either more weight is added or more sets and repetitions are performed. (Sets are the exercise groups, while repetitions are the number of times an exercise is performed.)

There are two forms of resistance training: traditional and circuit. Traditional involves doing one exercise at a time and completing the sets and repetitions for that exercise. For example, an exercise is performed 10 times, then there is a rest period of 30 to 60 seconds, 10 more exercise reps, then another rest and 10 more exercise reps: 3 sets of 10 repetitions each.

Circuit training involves numerous stations where different exercises are performed. An athlete moves from station to station, either doing a specific number of repetitions or performing the exercise for a specific period of time. This type of training adds variety to workout sessions.

With any type of resistance training, athletes usually make rapid gains during the first few weeks and then fall off to steady but less-apparent gains. Plateaus are common through this period, and moves from one step to another may take four to six weeks.

After successfully completing a resistance-training program, eliminating it for any length of time will cause a decrease in muscle strength, power, and endurance. For this reason it is important to maintain training even during the swimming season. As pool workouts are increased, however, resistance training can be reduced to accommodate the needs of the time period.

Just before a race, a swimmer should not do strenuous resistance workouts. At this time, he or she can taper resistance training to a maintenance level. (See chapters 6 and 8 for more about tapering.)

Three-Phase Approach

The most successful training programs used by swimmers in the United States combine in-water workouts with dryland resistance training. S.P.O.R.T.'s program uses three distinct time periods for this training: off-season or phase 1 for 2½ months; pre-season or phase 2 for 1½ months; and in-season or phase 3 for 1 month. The swim-training parts of this three-phase approach are covered in chapter 8, "Designing a Training Program."

For resistance training, the three-phrase approach works like this:

Phase 1—strength training. This is the foundation of all the other phases of resistance training. For 2½ months the athlete lifts heavier weights or uses more resistance on machines and exercise devices—all at a fairly low number of repetitions. The object is to build muscles that surround the shoulders, arms, hips, and knee joints. This added strength will improve performance and aid in preventing injury.

Phase 2—power training. The most important resistance training for swimmers emphasizes power. For the next 1½ months, the athlete is concerned with speed and explosive movements. For this, lighter weights are used, but there are more repetitions performed in a fast, dynamic manner. The strength of phase 1 is now combined with speed: power = strength × speed.

Phase 3—endurance/power training. As peak performance approaches, endurance and power are combined by using an increase in the number of repetitions plus resistance or weight. The weights are light enough to permit movement speeds duplicating the high turnover rate of strokes.

Efficiency Tips

- Workout sessions should be 45 to 60 minutes, 3 times a week.
- **Allow at least 24 hours between resistance sessions to give muscles time to build and repair themselves.**
- Be sure to warm up before training sessions and cool down after.
- Intensity and consistency are the most important factors in increasing strength, power, and endurance.

In-Water Resistance Devices

Some of the devices described in chapter 2, "Swimming Equipment," can be used for resistance training during swimming workouts. These devices should not be used instead of dryland resistance training, but may enhance it or help a swimmer with specific problems.

Hand paddles, for instance, increase the surface area of the swimmer's hands, providing more resistance to work the muscles of the hands, arms, shoulders, and back. The greater leverage provided by this device also permits swimming at a faster pace.

Kickboards and fins isolate kicking motions, giving added resistance to leg and hip muscles. Pull-buoys isolate stroke movements, giving added force to arm and shoulder muscles.

Such in-water devices are useful in serving two purposes: resistance training and the duplication of swimming motions.

Resistance Training Equipment

Four sources of resistance-training aids are available to athletes: body weight, free weights, machines, and surgical tubing resistance devices. All of these resistance sources have specific advantages, but ideally, for variety and change of pace, they should be combined for the best strength, power, and endurance training.

Body weight or self-resistance is used in push-up, sit-up, and pull-up exercises. Readily available items such as towels and a length of rope can make body-weight exercises with a partner even more valuable, and chairs or benches can be used for push-up or triceps dips between them. Where incline boards or stomach wheels are available, these too can increase the productivity of self-resistance exercises. A partner can help with training by adding resistance for many exercises in this category.

Free weights offer an endless variety of exercises and allow for a full range of motion during practically any resistance exercise a swimmer wishes to do. The Olympic standard barbell with a revolving bar and dumbbells with revolving sleeves are the most efficient free weights. Accessories for free-weight workouts are benches and weight racks, belts, gloves, and grip straps. Athletes should get professional instruction in the use of free weights and use a spotter when lifting barbells and other very heavy weights that could cause injury.

Resistance-training machines come in a broad range of styles and are widely available in fitness centers and school gyms. Some use stacks of weights that an athlete moves with a chain or pulley and a cam to keep resistance steady. Others have hydraulic or air-resistance features. A swim bench, used by some of the major swim centers, simulates swimming strokes against resistance. The disadvantage associated with most of these machine weights is that the body remains in a fixed position while the exercising limb or body part moves through a limited range. They are, however, safe and can provide training for specific muscles.

Surgical tubing resistance devices are made of a length of surgical latex tubing with adjustable hand and foot grips and an attachment that enables the device to be fixed to a doorjamb. The S.P.O.R.T. Cord is the most sophisticated of these devices and is used by many elite amateur and professional athletes. The main advantage of using the S.P.O.R.T. Cord for exercise is that a swimmer can duplicate swimming stroke motions with varying amounts of resistance. It is also useful as a rehabilitation device following injuries because of the infinite amount of resistance that can be applied. **The S.P.O.R.T. Cord is light and portable and is inexpensive when compared to other resistance-exercise equipment.** For information about this device, write to S.P.O.R.T. Cord, Inc., P.O. Box 731004, South Lake Tahoe, CA 95731, or call (916) 541-6961 (CA) and (800) 327-2673 (outside of CA).

Total Body Exercises

The exercises outlined on the following pages involve the total body rather than specific parts of the body that might seem to relate to a particular sport. This is because, although a sport such as swimming involves primarily the upper body, swimmers also use the lower body and need total body balance. They can build up the muscles that are used most in swimming by doing more repetitions and working at greater intensities on those body parts.

Swimmers should, for instance, stress the latissimus muscles of the back and the triceps to develop pulling motions in strokes. The hip flexor and extensor muscles are also used in swimming, as are the adductor and abductor muscles of the legs, and these, too, should get special emphasis in resistance training. The half-squat and power cleans with a barbell are excellent ways to develop power and endurance as well as total body strength.

Ultimately, the swimmer who can combine strength, power, and endurance with the correct technique has the greatest advantage in meeting personal challenges and in winning competitions.

Suggested Resistance Exercises

Order of Exercises

S.P.O.R.T. CORD
SRD
Warm-up
Lat pulls
Standing french press
Arm curls
Upright rowing
Seated leg press
Hamstring strider
Outside-inside leg toners
Gluteal strengtheners
Hip pulls
Sit-ups
Cool-down

MACHINE/FREE WEIGHTS
Warm-up
Lat pull-down
Barbell upright rowing
Barbell triceps curl
Barbell curl
Seated leg extension
Hamstring curl
Barbell half-squat
Power clean
Incline board sit-ups
Cool-down

Lat Pulls

Using the S.P.O.R.T. Cord, attach the cord to a doorjamb and assume a standing lunge position facing the door. Use a straight arm pull through the full range of motion and repeat the exercise.

Muscle group: Latissimus—large muscles on the back			
PHASES:	OFF-SEASON	PRE-SEASON	IN-SEASON
Sets	3	4	2–3
Reps	8–10	10–15	25

Standing French Press

With a S.P.O.R.T. Cord place the cord low in a doorjamb and bend your elbows with hands behind your head. Extend the arms to work triceps in isolation.

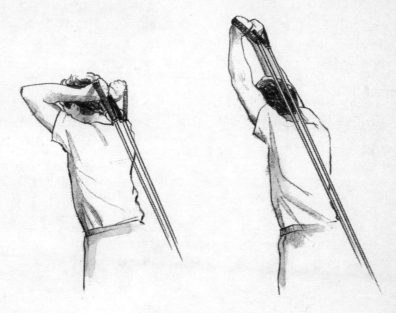

Muscle group: Triceps—muscles on back of upper arm			
PHASES:	OFF-SEASON	PRE-SEASON	IN-SEASON
Sets	3	4	2–3
Reps	8–10	10–15	25

Arm Curls

With a *S.P.O.R.T.* Cord place your feet on the cord wider than shoulder width. Knees should be slightly bent. Keeping your elbows close to the sides of your body, slowly bend arms at the elbows and curl toward shoulders. Alternate arms while performing the exercise.

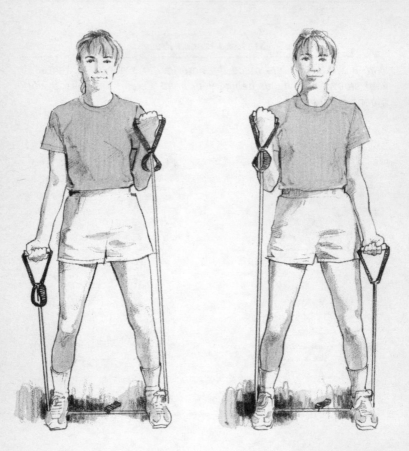

Muscle group: Biceps—muscles on front of upper arms			
PHASES:	**OFF-SEASON**	**PRE-SEASON**	**IN-SEASON**
Sets	3	4	2–3
Reps	8–10	10–15	25

Upright Rowing

While standing on the S.P.O.R.T. Cord, grasp the handles at waist level. Pull the handles toward your chin.

Muscle group: Deltoids and trapezius—muscles on the front of shoulders and top of upper back		
PHASES: OFF-SEASON	PRE-SEASON	IN-SEASON
Sets 3	4	2–3
Reps 8–10	10–15	25

Seated Leg Press

Using a S.P.O.R.T. Cord begin by holding on to the cord with your hand. Put one foot through the handgrip attachment and flex your knee. Extend the knee by pushing down and away from your hand. There should be a slight bend at the knee after completing the exercise.

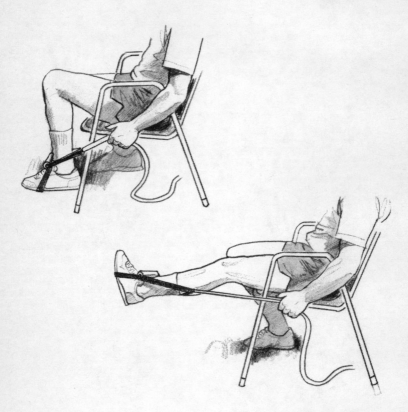

Muscle group: Quadriceps—large muscles on front of upper thigh			
PHASES:	**OFF-SEASON**	**PRE-SEASON**	**IN-SEASON**
Sets	3	4	2–3
Reps	8–10	15	25

Hamstring Strider

The door attachment of the S.P.O.R.T. Cord is placed in a doorjamb. Put one foot through the handgrip attachment and extend it in a forward stride position. Slowly bend your knee and curl your leg backward. The heel of your foot will move toward or touch your buttocks.

Muscle group: Hamstrings—large muscles on back of upper thigh		
PHASES:	OFF-SEASON	PRE-SEASON	IN-SEASON
---	---	---	---
Sets	3	4	2–3
Reps	8–10	15	25

Outside-Inside Leg Toners

Attach the S.P.O.R.T. Cord to the lower part of the doorjamb. Place
your feet shoulder width apart while resting a hand on a chair for
balance. To tone the inside leg muscles, place foot strap on your
inside foot. Keeping your inside leg straight, slowly draw your leg in
front of your outside leg. To tone the outside leg muscles, place the
cord on your outside leg and slowly raise it laterally as far as range
of motion permits. Repeat exercises on the opposite leg.

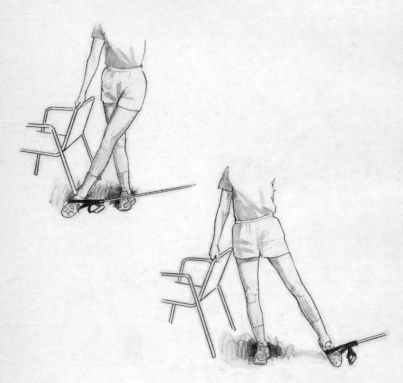

Muscle group: Adductors and abductors—muscles on the inside and outside of the thigh		
PHASES:	**OFF-SEASON**	**PRE-SEASON**	**IN-SEASON**
Sets	3	4	2–3
Reps	8–10	15–20	25

Gluteal Strengtheners

Attach the S.P.O.R.T. Cord to the lower part of a doorjamb. Facing the door, step through the handgrip attachment and slide the handgrip to a position above your knee. Place one hand on a chair for balance. Pre-stretch the cord by stepping backward with a backward lunge position. With bent knee, kick back as high as possible using a dynamic motion.

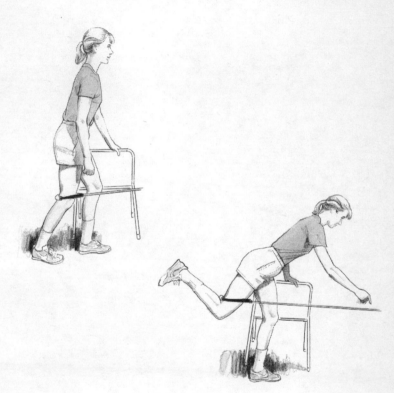

Muscle group: Hip extensors—muscles on the back of the hip			
PHASES:	**OFF-SEASON**	**PRE-SEASON**	**IN-SEASON**
Sets	3	4	2–3
Reps	8–10	15	25

Hip Pulls

Attach the S.P.O.R.T. Cord to the lower part of a doorjamb. Facing away from the door, step through the handgrip attachment and slide the handgrip to a position above your knee. Place one hand on a chair for balance. Prestretch the cord by stepping out into a lunge position. Raise your exercising leg as high as possible in a dynamic motion and return to original position.

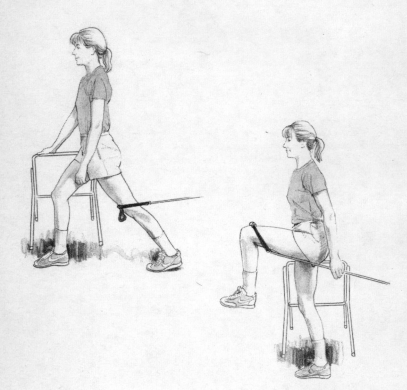

Muscle group: Hip flexors—muscles on the front of the hip		
PHASES:	**OFF-SEASON**	**PRE-SEASON** **IN-SEASON**
Sets	3	4 2–3
Reps	8–10	15 25

Sit-ups

With your knees bent at about a 45 degree angle, clasp your hands behind your head. Slowly curl your upper torso to your knees and return to your starting position. It is important to keep your feet in a fixed position. Variations to the full bent-knee sit-up are quarter or half bent-knee sit-ups.

Muscle group: Abdominals—stomach muscles			
PHASES:	**OFF-SEASON**	**PRE-SEASON**	**IN-SEASON**
Sets	3	3	3
Reps	25–30	30–40	40–50

Lat Pull-down

This exercise can be performed using a pull bar in a kneeling or seated position. Using a wide grip for a full range of motion, pull the bar down behind your head to the shoulders.

Muscle group: Latissimus—large muscles on the back			
PHASES:	*OFF-SEASON*	*PRE-SEASON*	*IN-SEASON*
Sets	3	4	2–3
Reps	8–10	10–15	25

Barbell Upright Row

In a standing position with your arms straight, raise the barbell toward your chin. Use a narrow to medium grip.

Muscle group: Deltoids and trapezius—muscles on the front of shoulders and top of upper back			
PHASES:	**OFF-SEASON**	**PRE-SEASON**	**IN-SEASON**
Sets	3	4	2–3
Reps	8–10	10–15	25

Barbell Triceps Curl

While lying on your back, slowly lower the barbell until it is close to your forehead, then raise it to a straight-arm position. A narrow to medium grip should be used.

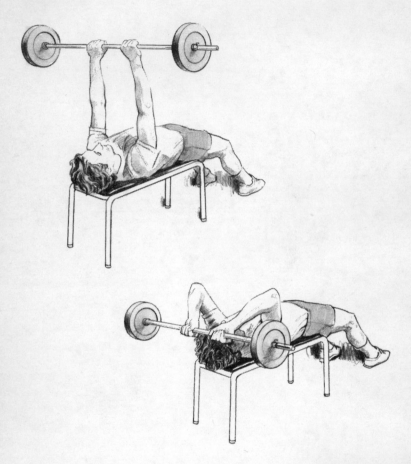

Muscle group: Triceps—muscles on back of upper arm			
PHASES:	**OFF-SEASON**	**PRE-SEASON**	**IN-SEASON**
Sets	3	4	2–3
Reps	8–10	10–15	25

Barbell Curl

With arms extended, curl the bar toward your chest. Use a medium-width grip with palms up.

Muscle group: Biceps—muscles on front of upper arm			
PHASES:	*OFF-SEASON*	*PRE-SEASON*	*IN-SEASON*
Sets	3	4	2–3
Reps	8–10	10–15	25

Seated Leg Extension

Using a leg machine, raise your lower legs until they are fully extended. There should be a slight bend at the knee after completing the exercise. Lower your legs slowly upon return to the starting position.

Muscle group: Quadriceps—large muscles on front of upper thigh			
PHASES:	**OFF-SEASON**	**PRE-SEASON**	**IN-SEASON**
Sets	3	4	2–3
Reps	8–10	15	25

Hamstring Curl

Using a leg machine, raise your lower legs toward your buttocks, working them one at a time. Lower slowly eccentrically to the starting position.

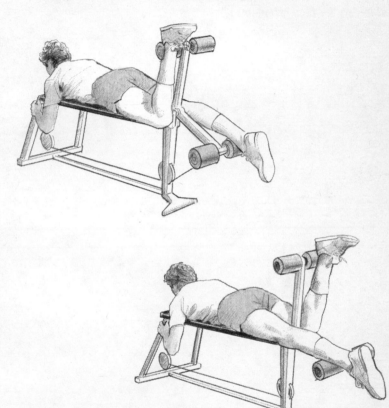

Muscle group: Hamstrings—large muscles on back of upper thigh			
PHASES:	**OFF-SEASON**	**PRE-SEASON**	**IN-SEASON**
Sets	3	4	2–3
Reps	8–10	15	25

Barbell Half-Squat

To do half-squats use a power rack and a "spotter." Keep your head up and your back straight as you perform this exercise. This exercise is best performed with an Olympic barbell, and you should have proper instruction and supervision. It is not recommended for athletes with back problems.

Muscle group: Quadriceps, hamstrings, back and hip extensors—muscles of the front and back of upper thigh and back of the hip			
PHASES:	OFF-SEASON	PRE-SEASON	IN-SEASON
Sets	3	3–4	4
Reps	6–8	10–12	12–15

Power Clean

With your head up and back straight, try for a good high pull before bringing your body back under the bar. This exercise is best performed with an Olympic barbell, and you should have proper instruction and supervision. It is not recommended for athletes with back problems.

Muscle group: Upper and lower body muscles			
PHASES:	**OFF-SEASON**	**PRE-SEASON**	**IN-SEASON**
Sets	3–4	4	3
Reps	6	6–8	8–10

Incline Board Sit-ups

With your knees bent at about a 45-degree angle, clasp your hands behind your head. Slowly curl your upper torso to your knees and return to your starting position. An incline board allows you to vary the resistance by raising or lowering the board.

Bent-knee sit-ups can be performed without using an incline board. For best results, place your feet under a table or sofa. Variations to the full bent-knee sit-up are quarter or half bent-knee sit-ups.

Muscle group: Abdominals—stomach muscles			
PHASES:	*OFF-SEASON*	*PRE-SEASON*	*IN-SEASON*
Sets	3	3	3
Reps	25–30	30–40	40–50

CHAPTER 6

CARDIOVASCULAR PATHWAYS

The human body has three distinct metabolic pathways that are the main energy sources for all activity, but are particularly critical for athletic activity. A swimmer can get more out of training sessions by understanding how these metabolic pathways affect muscles and which ones apply specifically to his or her competition events and recreational swimming preferences.

One of the three pathways, the aerobic, has become familiar to athletes in recent years because of its importance in long-distance running events and recreational jogging. Endurance sports like these rely on oxygen for continuous energy over long periods of time, and a well developed aerobic pathway carries abundant amounts of this major energizer to muscles involved in the activity.

The two other pathways, both anaerobic—meaning that they do not require oxygen—are less well known among recreational athletes, but are no less vital than the aerobic pathway. These two pathways are the energy suppliers for sprints and other short-duration sports events. The lactic acid pathway and the ATP-PC pathway do not use oxygen as an energy source, but rather involve other processes to provide muscles with fuel for rapid contractions.

The aerobic and anaerobic pathways may overlap in efficient athletic performance during many events. More often, however, one or the other pathway is predominant for a particular event and therefore should be emphasized in training sessions.

APPROXIMATE PERCENTAGE OF AEROBIC AND ANAEROBIC ENERGY PATHWAYS REQUIRED FOR DIFFERENT SWIMMING EVENTS

Event (meters)					
50	100	200	400	800	1500
•	•	•	•	•	•

Anaerobic 100% 90 80 70 60 50 40 30 20 10 0% Anaerobic

Aerobic 0% 10 20 30 40 50 60 70 80 90 100% Aerobic

Anaerobic energy pathway ——
Aerobic energy pathway ------

Adenosine triphosphate (ATP) is a chemical form of energy found in muscles and is the basis for all muscle contractions. Different events—endurance, middle distance, and sprints—utilize ATP in varying amounts, which means athletes can anticipate ATP usage and train accordingly.

During long-distance events, for instance, the aerobic pathway enables a well-trained athlete to sustain exercise for very long periods. The metabolic system in this instance is able to produce an almost unlimited supply of ATP to meet the requirements of muscles over this long time span. Furthermore, the aerobic pathway carries no end products that can cause immediate fatigue or muscle-contraction problems in athletes who are trained for endurance events.

The ATP energy required for the aerobic pathway is derived

from the breakdown of carbohydrates, fats, and, to a lesser extent, proteins. Carbohydrates supply two important fuels for exercise: blood glucose or sugar and muscle glycogen, a complex form of glucose. Fats, which are vital in ATP production, are carried in the blood as free fatty acids (a chemical form of digested fat) and are stored as muscle triglycerides (stored fatty acids). Other important sources of fuel are the liver for glycogen and storage fat for triglycerides.

The second pathway, the anaerobic lactic acid pathway, uses glycogen from muscles in addition to the ATP-PC pathway for an all-out effort lasting 45 seconds to 2½ minutes. This intense effort results in an incomplete breakdown of the muscle glycogen, which produces lactic acid. As the lactic acid builds up in the blood and muscles, it eventually interferes with muscle contraction and causes fatigue.

The third pathway, the ATP-PC pathway, is also anaerobic and is the only pathway that does not use a fuel, such as glycogen, as an energy source. ATP is available in the muscles for immediate use. The PC in the name stands for phosphocreatine, another chemical compound found in muscle cells that aids in the reformation of ATP. This process enables athletes to reach maximum peak performance for extremely short events of ten seconds or less.

Both anaerobic pathways are more rapid in supplying ATP than the aerobic pathway, but the ATP supply has a short duration. The lactic acid pathway also may be used in longer events that require a final kick of maximum effort and can produce the same muscle fatigue that is evident in shorter events.

Swimmers with knowledge of their own metabolic needs should use training sessions to develop one pathway more than the others. At the same time, it is important to realize that there is a cross-over in these pathways, so training sessions should include some elements of all three metabolic pathways.

Training the Metabolic System

The final goal in an efficient swimmer's training program is the optimum development of the aerobic-anaerobic systems. The swimming technique, the flexibility, and muscle strength are building blocks in achieving swimming proficiency—as well as the basis for realizing the maximum energy requirements needed for aerobic and anaerobic workouts.

Depending on the frequency, duration, and intensity of workouts, changes occur in an athlete's heart, lungs, blood, and muscle tissue as a direct result of training. The heart rate, for example, decreases at rest, so instead of the normal 70 to 72 beats per minute, it may be as low as 60 to 66 beats per minute. This training effect indicates that the heart has become stronger, capable of pumping more blood using fewer beats per minute. This is because there is an increase in the diffusion of oxygen from the air to the lungs and from the lungs to the heart. In other words, oxygen is finding a more efficient way to get into the bloodstream. In addition, the amount of blood pumped per heartbeat increases at rest and during exercise, which aids in getting a better supply of oxygen and nutrients to the working muscles. As a training program continues, an athlete can expect increasing amounts of oxygen to be extracted from the blood by the contracting muscles.

The end result of aerobic training is an increase in the body's efficiency to move oxygen to the lungs, from the lungs to the heart, from the heart to the blood, and then to dump that oxygen into the exercising muscles. This end result allows the muscles to respond as needed during athletic performance. Aerobic training includes middle-distance, distance, and ultradistance specialties. Swimmers in these disciplines should emphasize the development of a sound aerobic base before beginning training programs that use higher intensity, speed-oriented workouts. With a good aerobic foundation, swimmers have time to concentrate on stroke and kick technique. Early in the season, all swimmers should use some form of aerobic training, but this training should be monitored according to distance specialties.

During aerobic training, physiological changes take place in the muscles as glycogen and triglycerides increase and slow-twitch muscle fibers increase in size. Such changes occur to a greater or lesser extent depending on individual anatomy and predisposition, but at least six weeks are needed before changes become evident.

Anaerobic training develops the energy pathways for sprint and middle-distance swimmers by enhancing rapid muscle contraction. This training consists of higher intensity but shorter exercise sessions than those of the distance swimmers, with more emphasis on stroke turnover rate using good technique as well as speed and power. Distance swimmers, however, often use anaerobic training in workouts to promote turnover and power in strokes. Anaerobic training can be used one to two times per week in phases 2 and 3. Never do two consecutive days of anaerobic training.

Physiological changes that accompany anaerobic training include an increase in muscle-fiber diameter of fast- and slow-twitch muscles, with a somewhat greater increase in the fast-twitch fibers. In addition, anaerobic workouts help athletes tolerate the lactic acid build-up that causes fatigue. The secret is to create a higher and higher lactic acid threshold so that the detrimental lactic acid build-up occurs later and later during intense workouts. Gradually higher and higher levels of lactic acid can be tolerated before fatigue sets in.

Swimmers should closely monitor these high-intensity workouts because they can result in poor swimming technique, extreme fatigue that leads to incomplete workout sessions, and general psychological staleness. The anaerobic pathways usually can be adapted faster through training than can the aerobic pathway.

One way to control anaerobic threshold training is to think of it as an advanced form of aerobic training. This means regulating the workouts to just below or at the threshold and not beyond to a zone where there is an increase in lactic acid accumulation that eventually terminates the workout.

Once a swimmer has decided on which distance to specialize, he or she must use training methods to build up the cardiovascular system to meet the needs of that specialty. By being aware that the energy-pathway requirements for sprinters, middle-distance, distance, and ultradistance swimmers are different but overlapping, basic distance ranges can be selected for appropriate metabolic training.

Sprints	—50 to 100 meters
Repeats	—100 to 400 meters
Intervals	—100 to 800 meters
Distance	—400 to 1,200 meters (or longer for continuous lap swimming and ultradistance)
Time trials	—near maximum pace at any distance

An effective training program should consist of at least two, preferably three, of these distance ranges. Each time a swimmer moves from one method to another, however, he or she should make a gradual, smooth transition to the new distance or technique so that the body will not experience undue stress.

At the beginning, a sprinter should cover 1,000 to 2,000 meters per day, and distance swimmers should work toward 2,500 to 3,000 meters per day. At the elite level, sprinters cover 4,000 to 5,000 meters per day, while distance swimmers train for 15,000 to 20,000 meters per day.

To achieve the maximum aerobic or anaerobic benefits from each workout session, it is important to establish an individual base or foundation in training performance and then fine-tune each workout with specific goals in mind. Such fine-tuning does not necessarily mean more training or more meters each day, but rather training that involves more concentrated and intense workouts. The net effect is to slightly overload the skeletal and muscular systems, which may result in temporary and slight muscle soreness, but indicates progress.

Training Variables

Obviously, many variables must be weighed in order to achieve maximum benefits from a training program. The frequency of training should be at least three to five times per week and should be organized in advance—planned on a daily, weekly, and monthly basis. The duration of a training session depends on how much time an athlete can afford to spend as well as what he or she wishes to accomplish.

The intensity of workouts has several facets that need to be established and adjusted as training progresses.

Sets are the number of workout subdivisions with a prescribed rest between sets.

Repetitions are the number of times a particular distance or method is performed in a set or single workout session.

Time is the prescribed period for each repetition. It might be 100 meters, then a rest for 1½ minutes, and then repeat the 100 meters and rest periods 4 more times. Such a time period is phrased like this: 5 × 100 on 1:30.

Laps or distance can be used to set the parameters of a workout session. A swimmer might begin with 4 laps, rest, then swim 8 laps, rest, then do 12 laps, rest, and so forth.

Performance monitors are heart-rate measurements as explained in chapter 8, "Designing a Training Program."

Some training variables are more passive in performance but are still extremely important in the total mix. Rest, for instance, is the amount of time needed for recovery between sets and repetitions. Recovery can be an exercise of easy swimming, kicking, and pulling, which is an excellent means of removing lactic acid to revive fatigued muscles.

Warm-ups are also fairly passive compared to the actual workout session, but are essential in preparing energy pathways to achieve their maximum performance. A warm-up might be a 5- to 10-minute leisurely swim or a 5-minute dryland stretching program followed by a short, easy swim. Cool-downs after the workout session can follow a similar pattern with easy laps before leaving the pool. In this instance, heart rate and respiration can provide a way to measure readiness to quit.

Tapering is the reduction of the training workload in sets, repetitions, and intensity before a peak performance. How much and how fast to taper off and when to start the process have not been precisely defined in the world of swimming physiology, although research is being conducted to try to pinpoint these variables. Most swimmers rely on inner messages from their bodies and taper off according to individual needs. A rough measure is to ease off training one to two weeks prior to peak performance. Some swimmers completely stop training two to three days before peak performance, but this procedure should be carefully monitored. Studies have shown that a major portion of a swimmer's metabolic adaptations are lost in as little as one to four weeks of inactivity.

The Aerobic-Anaerobic Edge

In most competitions, swimmers hit the water with fairly similar abilities in technique and style. Before getting to the pool, each one may have trained muscles to achieve maximum strength, power, and endurance benefits. In fact, some swimmers may be significantly stronger than others.

Invariably in swimming competitions, however, the difference between the winner and the rest of the field is in cardiovascular development. This is what aerobic and anaerobic training is all about. The athlete who has done his or her homework—turning the laps, swimming the thousands of meters, repeating the endless sets—is the one who will have the most highly developed and efficient energy pathways to produce faster times on the scoreboard.

As in any sport, each swimmer must decide how much commitment he or she is willing to put into this vital aspect of training. There are individual differences, there are individual needs, and there are many different ways to do aerobic and anaerobic training. The important thing is to learn what works best for you and do it!

CHAPTER 7

EFFICIENCY SWIMMING TECHNIQUE

Anyone can achieve the best possible physical condition, even have a positive mental attitude, but without correct technique no one can swim efficiently. **Being in good shape but not swimming well can cause an athlete to become frustrated and disenchanted.**

Fortunately, in recent years technological advances in the science of movement have made it possible for athletes and coaches to separate and focus on the elements of proper sports technique, as well as to pinpoint weaknesses in a particular athlete's performance.

Biomechanics is the name given to this aspect of sportsmedicine, and special high-speed cameras and video equipment are the principal technological tools that make it possible. Detailed photographs and stop-action and instant-replay video permit frame-by-frame analysis of angular and linear motion in a sport; how athletes gain speed, distance, and acceleration; and other components of athletic performance. In swimming, for instance, it is possible to see the effects of outside forces on a swimmer's body during various movements. This information has verified the whip kick for propulsion in the breaststroke, rather than the frog kick, which used to be the standard motion.

It is through biomechanics that an athlete can make the many parts of the training pyramid, described in chapter 1, fit together so that there are no gaps or overlaps. Individually or with the help of a coach, he or she can identify parts of the swimming technique that need to be improved and then outline a regimen of practice and training to correct those weak elements. This is the efficient way to create efficiency swimming technique.

Biomechanic Phases

The most important biomechanical breakthrough in swimming has been the specific identification and separation of the phases of swimming motion: the catch or preparation phase, the sweep or propulsion/movement phase, and the recovery or end phase. Performing each phase correctly is the goal of efficient swimming, and the ability to see parts of strokes as separate phases allows swimmers to rehearse each component separately.

The most dramatic change in swimming technique, as a result of biomechanical study, affects the second or sweep phase of strokes. Most students of swimming motion, as well as coaches and elite swimmers, now believe that the maximum propulsion results from lifting forces. These forces are not achieved through pushing or pulling, but rather through circular or angular patterns with the limbs.

Another recent technical change occurred in stroke length. The swimmer's propulsion or forward movement is only as effective as his or her ability to sweep water backward. Longer strokes are possible when there is a minimum amount of body drag, so keeping the body and limbs high in the water has taken on a greater importance.

Kicks have long been recognized as essential for propulsion. Now it is realized that kick patterns assist in maintaining the swimmer's body position in the water, preventing drag. Changes in kick patterns have been devised to get maximum power while cutting down on drag.

Stroke frequency is also changing. The efficiency of the sweep and recovery phases of the stroke affect the arm-turnover rate. The precise placement of the arms during these phases is of vital importance.

Even the position of the hands and fingers has been established in a precise manner. The fingers should be held together, the palms shaped in a cupped position, and the wrists relaxed.

Different strokes have different speed potentials, with freestyle being the fastest, followed by the butterfly, the backstroke, and the breaststroke. Each stroke also has a different ratio of arm to leg use, and biomechanical analysis has clearly shown that the freestyle, backstroke, and butterfly use predominantly arms, while the breaststroke uses arms and legs almost equally.

Such information is interesting, but far more useful to the swimmer in training are the specific biomechanical applications to technique in each phase of each stroke.

Backstroke

This stroke is performed with the swimmer supine (lying on his or her back) with arms and legs extended. The waterline should be at ear level, while the head is tilted slightly forward.

Catch phase. In the first phase of the stroke, one arm reaches back beyond the swimmer's head but is not fully extended. The hand reaches for the water with the little finger entering first. The swimmer "grasps" the water 5 to 6 inches below the surface.

Sweep phase. The straight arm, which used to be popular in this phase of the backstroke, is no longer used by serious swimmers. In the initial sweep phase, the hand turns slightly downward after entering the water. The arm, which remains wider than shoulder width until the elbow reaches the waistline, moves backward as it makes a downward sweeping motion. The elbow bends gradually until it approaches the swimmer's waistline, where it is extended in the water so that the hand is thrust toward and slightly beyond the thigh. This movement creates the final propulsion during the sweep phase.

Recovery phase. As the hand passes the thigh, the arm is extended and is ready to be lifted from the water. The arm is kept straight and relaxed as the lifting motion is performed using muscles of the shoulder and upper arm. The hand does not have a specific position until the beginning of the catch phase when the little finger is extended to lead the stroke into the water again.

Breathing. The standard backstroke breathing pattern is one breath per arm stroke, and, because the swimmer is supine, rhythmic breathing can be natural.

Leg action. The flutter kick maintains the correct body position

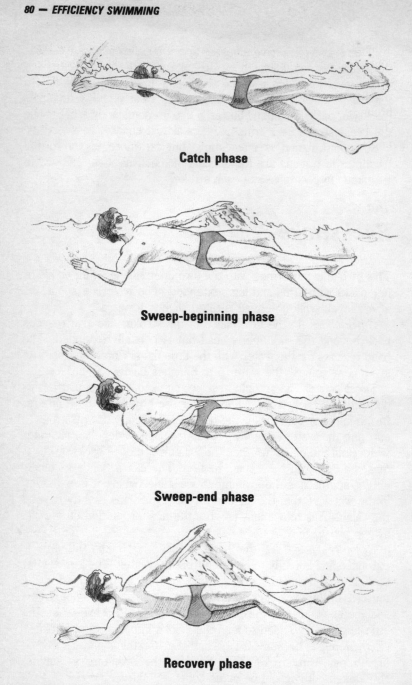

Catch phase

Sweep-beginning phase

Sweep-end phase

Recovery phase

Backstroke

in the water by buoying the center of gravity, preventing the legs from dragging. The muscles used for this kick are in the buttocks, hips, and thighs, while the feet are relaxed from the ankle joint. The knees undulate between a flexed and an extended position throughout the kick, with neither a full flexion nor a full extension. The legs are kept relatively close together, and kicking depth ranges from 10 to 20 inches. The normal cycle is six beats per two arm strokes or three beats per arm action.

Efficiency Tips

- There is a natural rolling of the body, but not enough to upset the correct position of the body.
- The head is relaxed in a semifixed position, and movement from side-to-side should be avoided.
- Correct breathing facilitates both of these important positions in the water.
- Kicking should also be quiet enough that there is not a large splash.

Breaststroke

In this stroke, the swimmer's body is in a prone position, lying on the stomach, with arms extended forward and legs backward. Usually the swimmer's head is in a forward position as the waterline is maintained at the same level as the eyes.

Catch phase. The arm stroke begins with a rotation of the wrists so that the swimmer's thumbs point down and the palms face outward. The arms move away from the body and prepare to grasp the water. This position should give the swimmer a feeling of "holding" the water.

Sweep phase. During the downsweep phase, the elbows begin bending as the hands move down and out in a circular pattern. Usually the elbows are kept higher than the hands, and the palms face backward. At this point the swimmer begins lifting his or her head for a breath. The circular pattern of the hands is completed as they are brought toward the body and positioned under the chest, allowing the elbows (which are 8 to 10 inches apart) to

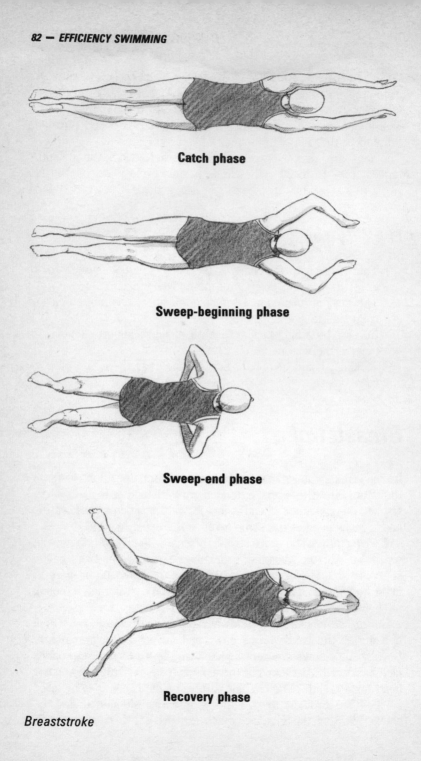

Catch phase

Sweep-beginning phase

Sweep-end phase

Recovery phase

Breaststroke

come near the body. Here the breath is taken. The hands are then angled toward the surface with the palms facing each other. This entire arm-sweep motion should be swift. A fast hand movement sets the tempo, and the final sweeping movement completes the propulsion portion of the stroke.

Recovery phase. After the hands come together, the arms are thrust forward in an extended position and the hands are placed 4 to 6 inches below the surface of the water, enabling the swimmer to maintain a proper body position. As the head is placed in the water for exhalation, there is a momentary glide just before the beginning of the next stroke.

Leg action. Propulsion from leg action is obtained from the whip kick, rather than the frog kick, which was popular in the past. In this action, the knees, held about shoulder width apart, are bent and the feet are drawn toward the buttocks during the catch phase. The toes are pointed outward and the soles of the feet backward. Legs are then extended outward and backward in an angular whip motion during the sweep phase. This explosive leg extension causes the whipping action as the feet move downward and inward. The key to this action is keeping the legs in a narrow plane during the catch phase, which sets up the power for the kick.

Recovery phase. At this point, the legs come together and there may be a momentary glide, although the current style is to begin the next stroke sequence without a glide in order to maintain maximum forward propulsion. This quick turnover is often seen in top-level competition.

Efficiency Tips

- Timing can be thrown off because of poor coordination between the arm strokes and leg action.
- When the kick or arm stroke sweep is not completed, there is a loss of propulsion force.
- Swimmers with previous knee problems should be alert for possible aggravation of those conditions caused by this kicking motion.

Butterfly

This stroke begins with the swimmer's body in an extended, prone position. Both arms are forward and move simultaneously during the stroke.

Catch phase. The hands enter the water about shoulder width apart with the thumbs pointing down, palms facing out. The elbows are held higher than the hands and may be slightly bent. The water is "caught" about 6 to 10 inches below the surface.

Sweep phase. A sweeping pattern in an "S" shape gains the most power and dynamic movement. The arms, with the elbows held a little wider than the shoulders, move out and down. About midway through the stroke, the hands gradually move from the thumbs-down entry position to a palms-down position as they grasp the water to begin the lifting motion. In this downsweep motion, the elbows gradually bend until they reach a 90-degree angle just below the chest. At this point, the hands come near one another with the palms facing down. Then the hands make an angular sweeping movement toward the thighs and finish the stroke past the thighs as the arms begin to extend. This portion of the stroke provides the maximum power.

Recovery phase. The hands and arms are lifted from the water. The arms are wider than shoulder width, and the elbows, which are higher than the hands, begin bending. At this point the hands lag behind the elbows in the swinging motion, but they are moving forward and will pass them before the catch phase. The arm recovery is relaxed but rapid enough to maintain rhythm and momentum. In the butterfly stroke, the greatest emphasis is on the shoulders and upper back, with the shoulders breaking the water surface during the recovery phase.

Breathing. Because of the strenuousness of the stroke, breathing on each arm stroke at the beginning of the recovery phase is the easiest technique when learning the butterfly. Lift the head up, take a quick breath, and return the head to the water for exhalation at the end of the recovery phase and the beginning of the catch phase. Later, breathing may be done on every other stroke or at other comfortable intervals.

Leg action. The butterfly utilizes a dolphin kick in which both

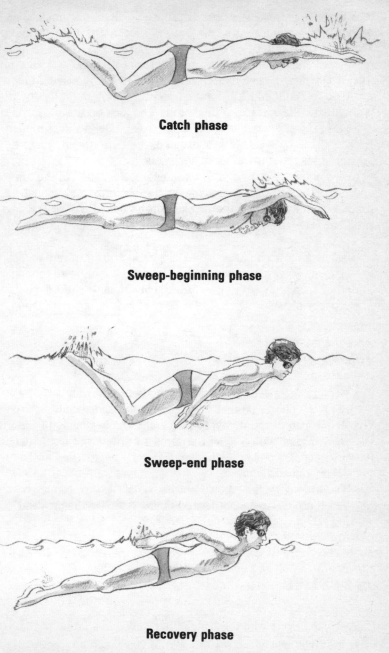

Catch phase

Sweep-beginning phase

Sweep-end phase

Recovery phase

Butterfly stroke

legs move in unison. The dolphin propels itself with an undulating motion that is simulated in the butterfly kick. The legs are held slightly apart with the knees slightly flexed and relaxed. The movement begins as the hips and buttocks rise and the kick is forced downward, and then continues as the hips and buttocks move down and the kick is forced upward. Very little of the lower body breaks the surface of the water. The kick occurs on a cycle of two beats per one complete arm stroke. This kicking motion is essential for power and propulsion in the butterfly and must be mastered for the most efficient technique.

Coordination of arms and legs. Simultaneous action of the arms and legs is difficult to coordinate in the butterfly and should be practiced regularly until the stroke can be added to the training program. The arm motion and the kick work together like this:

Beginning of catch phase   = dolphin kick in downward motion
Beginning of sweep phase   = dolphin kick in upward motion
End of sweep phase   = dolphin kick in downward motion
Recovery phase   = dolphin kick in upward motion

Efficiency Tips

- Be sure the sweep phase is finished before moving into the recovery phase, so that the stroke is not shortened.
- At the end of the recovery phase and the beginning of the catch phase, don't allow the arms to drift away from the body by becoming extended. Rather, begin the stroke action immediately.
- The kicking motion should not be too shallow or too deep, which can cause uncoordinated timing between the arm and leg action.

Freestyle

The stroke begins with the body outstretched in a prone position. The waterline is about level with the forehead.

Catch phase. The hand entering the water begins the catch

phase. The wrist is slightly bent, but relaxed, with the elbow lifted and the thumb in a downward position, palm facing out. The hand slides into the water as the arm is extended and reaches 5 to 6 inches below the surface.

Sweep phase. An "S" pattern in the sweep phase helps the swimmer take advantage of the body lift as he or she increases propulsion through the water. After the catch phase, the hand is rotated to grasp the water as it drifts slightly outward. The hand then moves inward as it sweeps down past the swimmer's chest. At the waistline, the hand begins an angular sweep movement toward the thigh and finishes past the thigh as the arm is fully extended. Acceleration is very important throughout the stroke, but just before the finish of the sweep, acceleration reaches a maximum.

Recovery phase. As the stroke is finished, the shoulder initiates the lifting of the arm, which is immediately followed by bending and lifting of the elbow as it moves forward. The hand lags behind the elbow, but catches up in the latter part of the recovery to start the cycle again.

Breathing. Freestyle calls for rhythmic and relaxed breathing. A breath is taken on one side with every other stroke, as the swimmer finishes the sweep phase and the opposite arm is beginning the catch phase. The head is rotated just enough for inhalation and then returned to the water for exhalation. After a swimmer masters the breathing pattern on one side, he or she should learn to breathe on the other side as well. Some top swimmers use this alternating breathing technique for competition.

Leg action. Propulsion with the legs is accomplished for the freestyle with the flutter kick. The legs move individually in an up-and-down motion—as one leg kicks down, the other kicks up. The legs are held relatively close together with the knees slightly bent and the feet relaxed from the ankle joint down. In this maneuver the muscles in the hips and thighs are utilized. Water depth for the flutter kick should be maintained at about 10 to 20 inches, because kicks that are either too deep or too shallow can waste power and energy. The cycle is six beats per two arm strokes, or three beats per arm action. This momentum, with the appropriate depth, should provide enough power to keep the legs from dragging in the water.

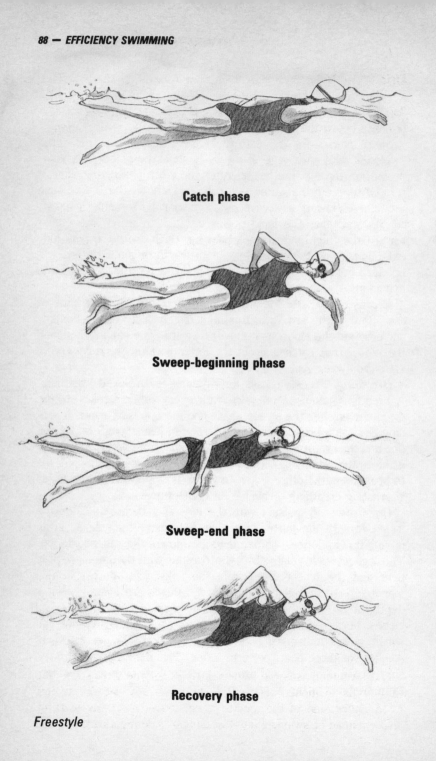

Catch phase

Sweep-beginning phase

Sweep-end phase

Recovery phase

Freestyle

Efficiency Tips

- Body roll or sway can work its way into the freestyle stroke motion. Be aware of this and watch for exaggeration in body movement.
- If the final portion of the sweep phase is not completed, power is sacrificed. Usually such incomplete action is caused by lifting the arms too early.
- Avoid dropping the elbow during the recovery phase, which allows it to drag in the water.
- The kick should be smooth in the water, causing only a minimum of surface turmoil.

Starts

Correct starts are important, not only for racing events but to compare swimming times in various strokes against those of top competitors. As with strokes, biomechanics has changed the style of starts from the shallow entry to the faster and more efficient pike position.

There are two types of racing dives in use today: the arm swing and the grab start. In either case, the goal is to direct momentum forward and out, rather than up or down. Swimmers should select the start style that seems most comfortable for their body type and mental set.

The body position for the arm-swing start is with the knees slightly flexed, weight on the balls of the feet and feet about shoulder width apart. The arms hang down in a relaxed position and the torso is flexed at the waist. The motion of the start begins by thrusting the arms backward and then immediately forward as the legs begin to extend. The swimmer's head is lowered during this extension phase of the dive. The final phase is an explosive push-off with the toes. The swimmer reaches for the water and gains momentum from the initial glide before the arm motion and kicking begin.

The swimmer uses the same principles for the grab start, but the body is positioned differently. The hands are placed between or on either side of the feet to grasp the edge of the starting block, instead of swinging into the motion. The knees are slightly flexed, weight forward and feet about shoulder width apart. The torso is bent at the waist. The motion of the start begins with an explosive extension of the legs as the body dives forward. The head is held down during this extension. Upon reaching the water, the swimmer has momentary gliding momentum before beginning the arm motion and kicking.

Turns

There are two distinct turning methods, and the nature of the stroke dictates which turn is used. The open turn is the easiest to learn and is used with the backstroke, breaststroke, butterfly, and freestyle strokes. The closed or flip turn is more advanced and can be used with the backstroke and freestyle strokes. It is also quicker to execute than the open turn.

The stroke used also determines hand touch in the turn. For the backstroke and freestyle open turn, one hand touches the wall, while for the breaststroke and the butterfly, two hands touch. The closed turn does not require a hand touch, but when used with the backstroke, a one-hand touch is necessary for proper execution of the turn.

Here are the steps in each type of turn:

Open turn. Touch with one or both hands. Immediately turn the body 180 degrees while drawing the legs in and planting the feet on the wall. With the legs in a tight, flexed position, release the hand or hands and then push off from the wall with a powerful extension of the legs. The arms and legs extend during the glide, and as it diminishes, the stroke and kicking begin.

Closed turn. In the freestyle stroke, the swimmer must judge the distance to the wall as he or she approaches in order to anticipate the beginning of the turn. The swimmer makes a front somersault movement simultaneously with a half-twist of the body. For the backstroke closed turn, the legs are drawn up and the body turns in a 180-degree spin motion. As one hand touches the wall, the legs are brought up over or around the shoulders. In both turns, as the feet touch the wall, the legs are coiled ready to spring away from the wall in a thrusting push-off. All of these actions occur very rapidly, so that the legs are actually coiling as the swimmer flips, rather than in a separate movement. After the turn, there is a brief glide and then the arm motion and kicking begin.

Effective Efficiency

With the advent of biomechanics, coaches and swimmers have become aware of an increasing number of variables in learning and mastering strokes. At the same time, technological improvements in training for muscle strength, power, and endurance can enhance the swimmer's ability to practice in-water skills. This synergism ultimately produces more effective and efficient swimming.

Each swimmer should realize, however, that the maximum potential for power, turnover rate, speed, and other skills is still an individual thing. That potential may be to learn the freestyle and then swim a comfortable 200 meters, or it may be to race against the clock for 200 meters. If you are not reaching your perceived potential, by all means get technical help from a coach or an expert.

CHAPTER 8

DESIGNING A TRAINING PROGRAM

Knowing what to do, how to do it, and why it is done are essential in achieving an efficient swimming technique. Reading up to this point, you should have become familiar with those building blocks of the training pyramid described in chapter 1. The next essential building block is the schedule or time frame on which to develop an efficient swimming program.

The most efficient and effective training takes place in cycles in which days, weeks, months, and seasonal phases are planned. It doesn't matter too much how the training sequence is scheduled—the three-phase approach described in this book is one way—but having a systematic organization to follow is vitally important. The swimmer in training must adjust his or her thinking and lifestyle to accommodate a regular program of workouts within a specific time frame to accomplish specific goals.

Obviously, such a disciplined approach needs to be weighed in relationship to personal considerations and time availability. Before creating a training program, swimmers must answer several questions:

1. What type of swimming—recreational or advanced—am I interested in?

2. How much time do I have available for training?

3. What training equipment is available to be included in my training program?

4. Following a check-up by a physician, are there any time limitations necessary because of health reasons?

5. What goals or objectives do I hope to achieve through swimming?

Another critical consideration in creating a training program is an evaluation of individual fitness. Fitness includes the level of technical swimming ability as well as the level of physical ability. Some athletes have trained their bodies for other sports and can carry over this fitness to swimming; some swimmers have learned the correct swimming technique more precisely than other swimmers. Beginning swimmers may be weak in both areas of fitness.

Fitness must also be considered in relationship to a swimmer's goals. Are they recreational or advanced—the first aiming for improved physical condition, the latter for sports performance achievements. A recreational swimmer can establish a training program that is somewhat flexible, using a schedule as a guideline rather than an exact time frame. On the other hand, an advanced swimmer who wants to qualify for the National Master's Swimming Competition must be much more rigid in adhering to a strict daily schedule. In either case, the controlling factor is individual initiative in carrying out the program.

The Program Outline

No matter what the ability level, athletes in training should have a yearly calendar on which to outline an individual training program. Such a program can be broken into three phases that build to a peak. Phase 1 might be called off-season and lasts for 2½ months. Phase 2 is pre-season and lasts for 1½ months. Phase 3 is in-season (the peak performance period) and lasts for 1 month. For advanced swimmers, this build-up must be specifically timed to a preset performance schedule, and it may need to be adjusted if this performance period is longer than 1 month with no break for additional training. **For recreational swimmers the three phases can begin again at the end of the third phase.** This

WEEKLY TRAINING SCHEDULE MODEL

Phase	Percent of Workout	Monday	Tuesday	Wednesday	Thursday	Friday	Saturday	Sunday
1 Off-season (2½ months)	10 20–25 55–60 10	Warm-up Resistance training Pool workout Cool-down	Warm-up Pool workout Cool-down	Warm-up Resistance training Pool workout Cool-down	Warm-up Pool workout Cool-down	Warm-up Resistance training Pool workout Cool-down	*Rest* or light pool workout	*Rest*
2 Pre-season (1½ months)	10 15–20 65–70 10	Warm-up Resistance training Pool workout Cool-down	Warm-up Pool workout Cool-down	Warm-up Resistance training Pool workout Cool-down	Warm-up Pool workout Cool-down	Warm-up Resistance training Pool workout Cool-down	*Rest* or light pool workout	*Rest*
3 In-season (1 month)	10 10–15 70–75 10	Warm-up Pool workout Cool-down	Warm-up Resistance training Pool workout Cool-down	Warm-up Pool workout Cool-down	Warm-up Resistance training Pool workout Cool-down	Warm-up Pool workout Cool-down	*Rest* or light pool workout	*Rest*

If possible, allow 4 to 6 hours between rigorous resistance training and a pool workout. This schedule must be adjusted if you begin to use workout sessions two or three times per week.

5-month program provides the athlete with the options to continue or change program planning.

Within each phase, swimmers can determine a workout schedule to practice events and strokes that interest them or what they want to do competitively. These should state specifically the sets, repetitions, distances, rest periods, and times for the core workout portion of the sessions as well as the water warm-ups and cool-downs.

Dryland warm-ups and cool-downs, which may not change through the three phases, need not be outlined on the schedule, but should be performed with 5 minutes of an easy aerobic activity followed by 10 minutes of stretching. This prepares the swimmer's muscles for the workout and prevents soreness, stiffness, and cardiovascular discomfort after workouts.

A swimmer in training should also prepare a weekly training schedule outlining daily dryland and water workouts as well as rest periods. The daily workout periods will change little within each phase, except for the amount of time spent in training, which may increase as the swimmer improves his or her swimming skills and body functions. The percentage of the workout time devoted to each part—warm-up, resistance training, pool workout, cool-down or rest—should remain the same throughout the training phase. An athlete who has limited time for swim training should reduce the amount of time spent on resistance training.

A recreational swimmer aiming to improve his or her cardiovascular system, rearrange body composition, and tone up muscles should plan daily workout sessions of 20 to 30 minutes for beginners and 45 for intermediates. Signs of improvements, however, may not be evident for 6 to 8 weeks into a training program.

Advanced swimmers usually want to upgrade their peak performance by swimming faster and longer with greater strength. In this case, a very high level of fitness is essential to begin with and must be maintained throughout the training program. At this level, a well-organized program requires daily sessions of at least 1 hour each and even longer for distance and ultradistance competitors.

Workout frequency is an individual matter, but definitely geared to a swimmer's objectives. **Recreational swimmers should train at least three to four times per week, while advanced swimmers should train at least four to five times**

per week. When other commitments prevent working out, it may be necessary to train twice in one day two times per week. Such twice-a-day workouts also may be beneficial for advanced swimmers during the second and third phases of training.

The Training Diary

A record of daily, weekly, monthly, and yearly performance for each athlete is a vital tool, not only to help in maintaining a training schedule but to show an athlete's growth and maximum potential. The training diary can be a simple notebook with entries for frequency, duration, distance, and intensity of each workout, or it can contain detailed charts of performance and other aspects of training. Obviously, advanced swimmers need more precise records than recreational swimmers use.

The most valuable logs are those that not only show progress on a daily basis but that are maintained throughout the day. Some of the items to record are:

Morning. Body weight, taken at least two times a week; heart rate; and sleep evaluated on a scale of 1 to 5, with 1 being poor and 5 excellent.

Dryland training. Resistance training should show each exercise performed as well as the number of sets, repetitions, and the amount of weight lifted. Training with specialized equipment, such as the S.P.O.R.T. Cord or a swim bench, should also indicate the number of repetitions and the amount of resistance.

Water workouts. Stretching and aerobic warm-ups should be indicated. The core training, in which strokes are practiced, should show the number of sets and repetitions, rest intervals, the amount of time devoted to swimming, kicking, and pulling, the heart rate, and the total distance covered. For cool-downs, the exercises should be recorded along with the amount of time devoted to each.

Injuries. Date, time, type, and cause of injuries should be recorded. Diagnosis of the injury can be indicated as well as rehabilitation procedures followed for a specific time period.

Nutrition. Dietary habits can be recorded and are especially important when there is a change in the food eaten or the timing of meals.

Rest. The exercising body needs periods or days of rest, and these should be recorded as faithfully as the exercising days.

Personal. Impressions, feelings, and observations about training and its effects on the athlete should be included in the training diary. Emotional highs and lows can be written down in detail whenever they seem significant.

The training diary need not be a chore, and it can be extremely useful in plotting progress and performance levels. Reading through it can be a reward in itself.

Workout Sessions

Work = Force × Distance. That is what athletic effort is all about—the force is the athlete constantly moving through a distance and expending energy. Aside from competitive events, workout or training (the words are used synonymously in this book) sessions are the times when this work takes place, whether on dryland or in water.

Wherever it takes place, each workout session should be designed so that the athlete is working at a percentage of his or her maximum ability. This maximum ability is called maximal level, which is the peak intensity or distance that an individual swimmer is capable of achieving. Conversely, submaximal levels describe swimming at a comfortable or easy pace rather than the deliberate act of swimming at a percentage of the maximum possible level. Cardiovascular maintenance workout sessions require at least a 70 percent effort.

Usually the percentage of maximal level is determined by using the training heart rate as a monitoring variable, because it indicates quite accurately how hard a person is working. The heart rate can be taken after sets or occasionally between repetitions and should be done often enough to establish an average or norm.

An athlete can determine his or her heart rate by lightly placing an index finger about 1½ inches to one side of the Adam's apple in the neck to feel the beating carotid artery. (Be careful—too much pressure on the carotid artery can cause a slowing of the heart rate due to a reflex action.) Using a watch or clock with a second hand, count the number of beats (each throb is a beat) for 10 seconds and multiply this number by 6. For example, a count of 15 beats in 10 seconds would be: $15 \times 6 = 90$ beats per minute. More accurate monitoring can be done with waterproof heart-rate watches to make aerobic and anaerobic training very productive.

To determine the intensity of a workout session, the maximum heart rate can be roughly estimated from a formula based on a cardiovascular study, keeping in mind that in reality this rate varies from swimmer to swimmer. Maximal heart rate decreases with age. The equation is:

$$Max\ HR = 220 - age$$

(Max HR is maximum heart rate.) Once this is established, the percentage of the maximal level can be estimated. For example, a 35-year-old man would have a maximum heart rate of 185. That is, $220 - 35 = 185$. His workout sessions could be based on these percentages:

Percent Effort	Training Heart Rate*
50–60	90–110
60–70	110–130
70–80	130–150
85–90	160–170
Near race-pace	175 or above

*Remember, when swimming the heart rate will be lower (10–15) beats per minute) compared to other types of aerobic activities (jogging, cycling, etc.).

In a cross-section of the population, the average resting heart rate has been determined to be approximately 70 to 72 beats per minute. With consistent training over a period of months or years, a decrease in this resting heart rate usually results. This is a great advantage to the cardiovascular system because it allows the heart to work more efficiently while at rest. A heart beating 55 times per minute is working much less than a heart beating 72 times per minute. If a swimmer wants to have an exact measure of his or her heart rate, a physician can do a graded exercise test that gives a scientific readout.

For the swimmer in training, the percentages of the maximal

level at which he or she needs to work depend on the preferred swimming categories and the training methods selected to improve those categories. Recreational swimmers may want to practice all types of swimming distances, but advanced swimmers usually select two or three to emphasize. Using a narrower scope allows an advanced swimmer to focus on problems, set specific goals, and monitor progress more easily.

There is more than one way to produce efficient swimming, but the sample in the following table represents a popular and successful approach.

TRAINING METHODS

Event	Swimming Distance	Predominant Energy Pathway	Training Heart Rate (Percent of Maximal Level)	Rest
Sprints	50–100 meters	Anaerobic	90–95%	Complete recovery
Repeats	100–400 meters	Anaerobic	80–90%	Not a complete recovery
Intervals	100–800 meters	Anaerobic or aerobic	70–85%	Not a complete recovery
Distance	400–1,200 meters	Aerobic	65–75%	Complete recovery
Time Trial	Any distance near race-pace	Anaerobic or aerobic	85–95%	Complete recovery

The training methods in the above table can be modified to fit the individual swimmer's needs and approaches. It is important, though, to include at least two of the swimming methods in each phase. For example, a sprinter should begin phase 1 (the off-season period of training) with endurance workouts to establish a sound base and gradually include more and more speed workouts until at phase 3 (the in-season training period) consists almost entirely of speed workouts at varying percentages of maximal level. The endurance swimmer should also begin phase 1 with endurance workouts with occasional faster workouts. Keeping the emphasis on endurance sessions, he or she should concentrate on getting faster through the use of improved technique at varying percentages of maximal level.

Measuring Progress

Specific training is needed by athletes of every ability in order to accomplish predetermined goals. To apply specific training it is necessary for swimmers to periodically review their strengths and weaknesses and then select training methods and equipment to work on those areas.

Usually recreational swimmers are content with cardiovascular, body composition, and muscular improvements, and training can be altered to work on these goals. Advanced swimmers may also be concerned with those goals, particularly the cardiovascular functions, but they can usually single out variables such as strokes, kicks, muscle strength, power, or endurance for specific improvement. While improving weaknesses, it is important to maintain existing strengths.

One way to improve the body's systems—skeletal, muscular, cardiovascular, and energy pathways—is to overload them during training. To do this, a swimmer establishes a basic workout routine as described in the Weekly Training Schedule Model on page 95. From this, he or she can delete segments of the training regimen in order to allow time to add or increase other training segments. For instance, after reaching a training plateau, one or more variables (such as intensity, sets, distance) can be increased. The objective is to improve the quality of swimming workouts in order to force the body systems to a higher plateau. Even with a very limited amount of training time available, improvements can be made through this overload principle, although it may take a very long time to become visible.

A recreational swimmer should start slowly when applying the overload principle, keeping his or her limitations in mind and gradually increasing elements of training. Advanced swimmers, who are more aware of their physical limitations and have had more experience with training programs, can push for greater distances and higher intensities more quickly and consistently. In either case, the objective should not be to create an increasingly demanding training schedule with more workout sessions per day or per week, but to improve within a set schedule. Moving to a more demanding schedule would necessitate a reassessment of an athlete's entire training program.

Progression is what every swimmer desires, but progress using the overload principle needs to be gradual, resulting in moderate changes in the body systems. For example, if you complete 5 × 100 meters in freestyle swims with 2-minute rests, the next day's objective should not be 15 × 100 meters with 1-minute rests. A more realistic overload would be 5 × 100 meters with 1:45-minute rests or 7 × 100 meters with 2-minute rests.

Tapering, described in chapter 7, is the opposite of overloading. In tapering, the workout sessions are gradually reduced before a major peak performance to allow the body to repair itself and be in top condition at the precise time of the competition. The best way to taper is simply to maintain regular workout sessions without overloading or pushing. This process may take place for just three days or as much as two weeks before peak performance. If there are preparatory races before major competitions, they should be viewed as training sessions rather than all-out performance events.

It is during periods when swimmers maintain regular workouts that they become aware that their bodies have adapted to the increasing demands placed on them. Such adaptation can be recognized and measured by comparing figures kept in a training diary showing there has been a weight gain or loss, an increase in muscle strength, a change in the cardiovascular system, or simply a different look to the body and muscles. This is a training effect and, when applied to swimming, usually it also reveals increases in speed or distance in the water. These adaptations take a minimum of six weeks to become noticeable and may not become evident for a much longer time, depending on the condition of the athlete prior to the start of training.

Psychological Hazards

Training too much has more serious consequences than not training enough. The athlete who overtrains usually has very high goals and is extremely determined, but too much work results in a feeling of being stale, listless, and without energy. He or she may even complain of lingering muscle soreness, have difficulty getting to sleep, and experience sudden weight loss. All of these may be signs of burn-out caused by unrelieved high-intensity training.

What is happening is that the body, like a finely tuned engine, is reacting to an overload. The first step in counteracting such overload is to recognize that it can and does happen—even to you! The next step is to analyze each segment of your training program and determine which variables—intensity, frequency, or duration—can be trimmed, while still maintaining the basic consistency of the program. Keep in mind that programs such as those outlined in this book are only suggestions and that each athlete must create a program that suits his or her individual physical condition, objectives, and mental approach. Even then, the program is not set in cement and can be adjusted and modified as time and conditions dictate.

Another way to counter overtraining is to plan daily workouts so that there are easy, moderate, and hard training sessions in an alternating pattern. For example, a week-long training schedule might look like this:

Day one   — hard workout

Day two   — easy or moderate workout

Day three   — hard workout

Day four   — easy or moderate workout

Day five   — hard workout

Day six   — light activity or rest

Day seven   — rest

If that seems too gentle for a determined athlete, an alternating workout program might look like this:

Day one — hard workout

Day two — hard workout

Day three — easy workout

Day four — hard workout

Day five — hard workout

Day six — light activity or rest

Day seven — rest

Whatever the form of the daily program, rest should be included as a part of the schedule. It is on rest days that the body has a chance to repair physical damage from training and the mind has a chance to recycle. Returning to training after a short rest period should feel like satisfying a newly created hunger.

Sometimes athletes are not overtraining but still they begin to lose interest in training and achieving goals. This may simply be boredom caused by too much sameness in the workout sessions.

Boredom can be relieved by adding variety to workouts. A sprinter, for instance, can add some middle-distance or even endurance sets to a weekly schedule. A distance swimmer can do sprints and shorter sets once or twice a week.

The point is to keep your goal in mind by doing most of the training for a favorite recreational or competitive event, but allow for a change of pace to make the program fun and interesting. **Altering a training program adds a new challenge and enhances appreciation of other swimming disciplines.**

Rest days also can be geared to relieve a feeling of boredom. Swimmers can try other sports that get them away from the pool environment and atmosphere, but such other activities should not leave an athlete feeling exhausted—just invigorated and eager for more swim training.

Male/Female Variations

For many years it was thought that women and men should pursue different training regimens in swimming and in practically every other sport. Recently, however, coaches and trainers have concluded that, for all practical purposes, men and women can train the same way up to each individual's potential. That means training programs differ little between sexes, but the results will vary because of differences in anatomical functions.

Male and female functional differences fall into four main areas: flexibility, body composition, strength, and cardiovascular potential.

Flexibility is very important in swimming, and, on the whole, swimmers are more flexible than other athletes. Within both sexes, some people are more flexible than others, but generally women are more flexible than men. Whatever an athlete's innate flexibility, this is one function that can be improved in both sexes through training.

"Body composition" refers to fat and fat-free weight. The important factor about an athlete's body composition is how much is fat versus muscle and bone, keeping in mind the fact that a low percentage of body fat does not necessarily produce outstanding performances. However, recreational and competitive athletes generally do have a lower percentage of body fat than does the general population. Nonathletic males have approximately 15 to 18 percent body fat, while nonathletic females have about 25 to 27 percent body fat. Among elite swimmers, the body fat ranges are 6 to 12 percent for males and 8 to 18 percent for females. Recreational swimmers generally have a lower percentage of body fat than nonathletic males and females.

Body fat can be estimated in a variety of ways, but two of the most popular methods in use are taking skin-fold measurements and doing hydrostatic underwater weighing. The calculations from these methods show precisely the percentage of body fat, fat-free weight, or lean body weight of an athlete and can even assist in calculating the ideal body weight. With this kind of information, a person can create a program to increase or decrease weight in specific portions of the body.

Hormonal changes experienced by women athletes may create

irregularity and, in some cases, an absence of menstrual periods. This menstrual change also may be due to a decrease in body composition, specifically a lower percentage of body fat and a reduction in total body weight. Other causes of menstrual changes may be the rigors of training, psychological stress, and even diet. Changes in menstrual patterns are not fully understood, but they are being studied.

Men have greater absolute (raw) strength than females, because they have larger muscles and more muscle mass. But when comparing relative strength values by separating the fat-free body-weight ratios, women are much closer in strength than is popularly thought. Furthermore, resistance-strength training is quite new among females, and as this training is pursued, relative differences diminish even more.

Within the muscle structure, the percentage of fast-twitch to slow-twitch fibers is approximately equal among men and women, but men have larger muscles and usually the fast-twitch fibers are the largest, allowing them to produce greater force during muscle contractions. Among women, a higher percentage of lean body weight is located in the lower torso, which explains why women's lower-body strength is closer to men's lower-body strength than upper-body strength. Other neuromuscular functions, such as nerve-to-muscle firing and reaction time, are not significantly different between men and women with comparable training and athletic ability.

Women have a lower cardiovascular potential than men do. With smaller bodies and a higher percentage of body fat, they cannot process as much oxygen, which results in lower maximal oxygen capabilities. Men have slightly larger hearts, which allow more blood to be pumped by the ventricles at each heartbeat. Therefore, men can get more blood with more oxygen to the muscles during maximal levels of exertion.

As women are exposed to better and more sophisticated training methods they are closing the gap on male performance levels. In fact, the times set by women in the 200-meter butterfly during the 1984 Olympics were faster than those for men in the same event for the 1968 Olympics.

EXAMPLE OF A THREE-PHASE
RECREATIONAL SWIMMING WORKOUT

	Phase 1 (off-season) 2½ months	Phase 2 (pre-season) 1½ months	Phase 3 (in-season) 1 month
Warm-up	1 × 200	1 × 200 1 × 100 pull	4 × 200 swim-pull-kick-swim
Core Workout	2 × 500 on 10:00 5:00 rest 1 × 200 pull 5:00 rest 1 × 200 kick	4 × 200 on 5:00 5:00 rest 4 × 100 pull-kick on 3:00	2 × 200 on 4:30 5:00 rest 6 × 100 on 2:30 5:00 rest 4 × 50 on 1:00
Cool-down	1 × 200	1 × 400	1 × 200 pull 1 × 200 kick

This example of a recreational workout is based on total meters of: 1,000 to 2,000 meters (40 to 80 laps).

The rest period will depend on the specific stroke used and the structure of the workout. The rest between repetitions depends on the aerobic or anaerobic workout design. In this example, the rest between repetitions is indicated (i.e., "on 5:00" means five minutes of rest).

Another popular method of integrating rest periods between repetitions is as follows: the workout asks for 5 × 100 on 1:45 and you swim the first 100 in 1:15; you have :30 seconds rest before you swim the second 100, etc.

This chart should assist you in understanding the phase changes. To maintain interest, use variety in your workout program. Anaerobic training sessions should not be on two consecutive days. The three examples of an advanced workout (sprint, middle-distance, distance) are based on total meters of: 1,000 to 2,000 meters (40 to 80 laps) for sprint and 2,500 to 3,000 meters (100 to 120 laps) for distance swimmers.

The rest period will depend on the specific stroke used and the structure of the workout. The rest between repetitions depends on aerobic or anaerobic workout design. In these examples, the rest between repetitions is indicated (i.e., "on 1:30" means 1 minute and 30 seconds of rest).

Another popular method of integrating rest periods between

EXAMPLE OF A THREE-PHASE
SPRINT SWIMMING WORKOUT

	Phase 1 (off-season) 2½ months	Phase 2 (pre-season) 1½ months	Phase 3 (in-season) 1 month
Warm-up	3 × 100 pull-kick-swim	2 × 200 pull-swim	4 × 100 swim-pull-kick-swim
Core Workout	5 × 200 on 3:00 5:00 rest 3 × 100 on 2:00	2 × 100 pull with paddles on 2:00 3:00 rest 2 × 100 kick on 2:30 3:00 rest 2 × 100 on 1:30 3:00 rest 10 × 50 on :40 5:00 rest 10 × 25 on :20	5 × 100 on 1:15–1:30 4:00 rest 3 sets of 5 × 50 on :35 with a 3:00 rest between sets 3:00 rest 10 × 25 on :15
Cool-down	3 × 100 pull-kick-swim	1 × 400	1 × 150 pull 1 × 150 swim

EXAMPLE OF A THREE-PHASE
MIDDLE-DISTANCE SWIMMING WORKOUT

	Phase 1 (off-season) 2½ months	Phase 2 (pre-season) 1½ months	Phase 3 (in-season) 1 month
Warm-up	1 × 200 individual medley 1 × 200	3 × 200 pull-kick- swim	5 × 100 pull with paddles
Core Workout	1 × 800 5:00 rest 3 × 400 pull on 6:00	3 × 100 on 1:30 4:00 rest 1 × 200 pull 2:00 rest 1 × 200 kick 2:30 rest 1 × 400 3:00 rest 1 × 200 pull 2:00 rest 1 × 200 kick 2:30 rest 3 × 100 on 1:30	4 × 100 on 1:15 5:00 rest 6 × 200 on 2:30 5:00 rest 4 × 150 on 1:45
Cool-down	1 × 400	1 × 500	2 × 200 pull-kick

EXAMPLE OF A THREE-PHASE
DISTANCE SWIMMING WORKOUT

	Phase 1 (off-season) 2½ months	Phase 2 (pre-season) 1½ months	Phase 3 (in-season) 1 month
Warm-up	1 × 400 individual medley	2 × 100 pull 2 × 100 kick 2 × 100 pull with paddles	1 × 100 pull 1 × 100 individual medley 1 × 100 swim 1 × 100 pull
Core Workout	2 × 500 on 8:00 6:00 rest 1 × 400 pull 5:00 rest 1 × 400 5:00 rest 1 × 400 pull 5:00 rest 1 × 400	4 × 200 on 2:30 4:00 rest 1 × 200 pull 2:00 rest 1 × 200 pull with paddles 2:30 rest 1 × 200 pull 2:00 rest 1 × 200 pull with paddles 2:30 rest 3 × 100 on 1:30–1:45	8 × 100 on 1:30 6:00 rest 1 × 400 time trial 6:00–7:00 rest 2 × 200 on 2:15 5:00 rest 2 × 400 on 4:00
Cool-down	3 × 150 pull-kick- swim	1 × 500	2 × 150 pull-kick 1 × 200 swim

repetitions is as follows: the workout asks for 5 × 100 on 1:45 and you swim the first 100 in 1:15; you have :30 seconds rest before you swim the second 100, etc.

These charts should assist you in understanding the phase changes. To maintain interest, use variety in your workout program. Anaerobic training sessions should not be on two consecutive days.

CHAPTER 9

EATING RIGHT

Nutritional planning is a natural and essential part of becoming an efficient athlete. Just as a swimmer organizes a training program, attends workout sessions, and keeps a training diary, he or she must eat correctly to keep body functions working at their maximum.

These days, that is not an easy task. The public is constantly being bombarded with books, magazines, and other publications that promote the latest and greatest diet systems. Some of these ideas are good, some are crazy, and some are just plain inaccurate.

The best way to sort the nonsense from the goodsense in creating a nutritional plan is to examine your dietary objectives and weigh them against conventional nutritional recommendations. The major objective for most athletes is to get more energy from food. A secondary objective may be to gain or lose weight. To accomplish these goals, you need to eat the right quality foods in appropriate quantities.

Begin nutritional planning by making a realistic appraisal of current food intake and estimate the number of calories you eat each day. Then, write down ways that this current diet might be improved and still stay within your time schedule and lifestyle. If this stymies you because you think you don't know much about food or nutrition, consult a registered dietician or nutritionist or ask a doctor for advice.

It is fair to guess, however, that most athletes know more about good eating than they think they do. The four basic food groups that most of us studied and memorized in grade school constitute a sound and dependable starting point for planning a well-balanced diet. Items from each of them—grains and cereals, fruits and vegetables, meat, and milk (lowfat) products—should be included in daily food intake.

Although the basic food groups have not changed, the recommended number of servings for adults has changed over the years.

SUGGESTED SERVINGS FROM THE FOUR FOOD GROUPS

	Milk (Lowfat)	*Meat*	*Fruit/Vegetable*	*Grain/Cereal*
Regular Diet	2	2	4	4
Training Diet	2	2	6–8	6–8

There may be individual differences in the number of servings and amount of food in each serving, but the above suggestions are a starting point for a sound daily diet. It is through the integration of nutrients from these four food groups that the body acquires the energy needed for maximum athletic gains.

Using Body Chemicals

The food we eat must be changed into chemical forms that can be assimilated into the body to provide energy, cellular growth and repair, metabolic functions, and many other systemic processes. Nutrients from the four food groups become the chemicals that make these processes possible.

Carbohydrates are nutrients made up of sugars and starches that are converted to chemicals called glucose and glycogen, which are glucose in its storage form. Some of the foods that provide carbohydrates are potatoes, rice, pasta, and grains and cereals. **Carbohydrates are not only the main source of energy for muscle activity, but are the most useful source because they are quickly available.**

Excess calories are stored in the body as fat in the form of fatty acids (a digested form of fat), which are then converted into triglycerides, the storage form of fat. As a source of energy, fats are more than twice as productive as carbohydrates and proteins, but they require more oxygen to be broken down for use. This means that the most productive use of fats is for endurance or distance training and competition.

Protein, a nutrient made up of amino acids, influences several body processes such as the production of enzymes and hormones, tissue repair, and muscle growth. It is not, however, highly significant in providing energy for athletes. Furthermore, excess protein not used for these processes is broken down and stored as fat.

For most adults, the recommended daily amount of protein is about .4 grams per pound per day. This is roughly the equivalent of protein found in one chicken breast weighing 3 to 4 ounces, one egg, ½ pint of lowfat milk, and 3 to 4 ounces of fish for a 160-pound swimmer. The amount of protein recommended for active athletes has been the subject of controversy, but evidence from tests and studies indicates that .4 to .6 grams is still adequate even for a hardworking exercising body.

Minerals are inorganic compounds such as calcium, phosphorus, potassium, and iron, also provided by food. These compounds are important for functions that include forming and repairing bones, which calcium does, and the formation of hemoglobin, which iron does.

Vitamins also come from foods and are vital in energy metabolism and other body processes. Fat-soluble vitamins, A, D, E, and K, are stored in the liver and in fatty tissue and are used as needed. Water-soluble vitamins, C and the B-complex group, must be constantly replenished by food. If the body receives more water-soluble vitamins than it needs, the excess is eliminated in the urine.

In recent years, the body's need for additional vitamins has been exaggerated, causing some athletes to consume large doses, even megadoses, to try to enhance performance. With water-soluble vitamins, such consumption has dubious value because the body eliminates any excess that it doesn't need. With fat-soluble vitamins, on the other hand, this practice can be dangerous. Large doses of these vitamins, especially A and D, can produce toxic effects that are extremely detrimental. In fact, in large enough quantities, even water-soluble vitamins can produce toxic results. Unless a doctor or nutritionist recommends supplemental vitamins, it is better to eat a well-balanced diet to acquire vitamins.

Water is also an important nutrient because the body is made up of 50 to 60 percent H_2O. Moreover, water is important in blood composition, food digestion, waste elimination, and the body's cooling process via perspiration. Athletes should consume plenty of water throughout the day, drinking at least 6 to 8 12-ounce glasses or even more, depending on the intensity and duration of training sessions.

Food is the source for all these nutrients, but not all foods provide nutrients in a beneficial form. Processed and fried foods may fill the stomach, but they usually don't add nutrients in a well-balanced manner. Refined sugars provide calories, but they are empty as far as providing nutrients for long-range benefits.

Complex carbohydrates, such as potatoes, pasta, brown or wild rice, and whole-grain breads and cereals are an excellent source of energy. Moderate amounts of chicken, fish, nuts, and legumes are adequate for protein nutrients. Unsaturated fats from olive oil and other vegetable sources are needed in very small quantities. Back up those food sources with large amounts of fresh fruits and vegetables, and you will have vast energy sources at your disposal. Fruit and vegetables are also an excellent source of fiber.

Fuels for Energy

Carbohydrates, fats, and, to a lesser extent, protein are the fuels for human energy. Understanding how each of them influences athletic performance can aid in determining nutritional needs.

Glucose from carbohydrates is used for energy, and excess amounts in the system are stored in the muscle and liver in the form of glycogen, which is many glucose molecules packed together. During moderate to high intensity physical exertion, carbohydrates are the main fuels consumed by the body. Workouts of light to moderate intensity use carbohydrates as well as fuel.

Fat is also called upon later during exercise because it takes approximately 20 minutes before the mobilization of free fatty acids from triglycerides, which are the storage form of fat, can equal or exceed the requirements needed by working muscles. While training, an athlete's fatty acid level increases in the blood plasma according to the rate of muscle-fiber utilization. In other words, aerobic training prepares the body for the consumption of this form of energy.

Protein supplies energy in limited amounts. Research has yet to determine what percentage of an athlete's energy is supplied by protein, but it is known that protein alone is not an adequate source of fuel for exercise.

An athlete's utilization of these fuels is dependent upon three training variables: frequency, duration, and intensity of workout sessions. Five exercise sessions a week, for the maximum length of time and at full capacity, can deplete the body's energy and be detrimental to performance.

Sprint-type, high-intensity swimming is anaerobic in nature and as such uses glucose and glycogen. If sprint workouts are frequent enough, long enough, and intense enough, glycogen stored in fast-twitch muscle fibers can be used up.

Middle-distance swimming is a combination of the anaerobic and aerobic energy systems. Calling on fast- and slow-twitch muscle fibers, middle distance swimmers can use up blood glucose along with stored glycogen and some free fatty acids.

Distance swimming is aerobic in nature, using glucose and glycogen as the main fuels for slow-twitch muscle fibers in a long exercise or competition. As the training or event continues, more and more energy is derived from free fatty acids that the body metabolizes. Again, excessive training can result in poorer performance.

In order to maximize the glycogen content in the muscles in sprint and middle-distance swimming, periodic high-intensity swims at or near maximum levels will maintain or enhance this energy store.

Endurance training at less than 70 to 80 percent of a swimmer's peak performance level (100 percent) depletes glycogen from the slow-twitch muscle fibers. After a period of time, this results in muscle fatigue and exhaustion. Some research indicates that this kind of training coupled with diet also produces a "glycogen sparing" effect in which an elevated enzyme activity of free fatty acids causes the body to use fats before all the carbohydrates are consumed. This means that glycogen stores are saved for later in the event.

Different time frames are required to replenish the three energy fuels. Fat is stored in the body and maintains a certain level despite exercise demands, and little protein is used as an energy source during exercise. On the other hand, muscle glycogen, which is the main energy source for athletes, needs to be replenished on a daily basis through consumption of complex carbohydrates (breads, fruits, vegetables, pasta, grains, and other sources mentioned earlier). Simple carbohydrates from sugar, honey, and other sweets can help in replenishment, but they do not contain valuable B vitamins found in the complex carbohydrates.

Restoration of glycogen does not occur immediately after strenuous training or competition. Athletes doing two workouts a day or three or four hard workouts in a row can experience glycogen depletion that reaches critical levels. Usually about 24 hours are needed to bring glycogen levels back to normal, but for ultradistance swimmers, 40 to 48 hours may be needed to replenish the muscles.

Dryland resistance training also consumes vital nutrients and this must be figured into a replenishment diet. All of these factors should be calculated into the dietary needs of a working athlete.

EXERCISE VARIABLES, NUTRIENTS, AND MUSCLE FIBERS

Training Methods	Intensity	Duration (Meters)	Carbohydrates Fats (Approximate Percent Utilization)		Slow Fast (Predominant Muscle Fiber)	
Sprint	Anaerobic	50–100	90–100	—	—	X
Middle Distance	Anaerobic and Aerobic	200–400	80–90	10–20	— X	— X
Distance	Aerobic	1500	70–80	20–30	X	—
Ultradistance	Aerobic	Open water, triathlon	Initial Stages: 60–70 30–40 Later stages: 30–40 60–70		X	—

Energy Expenditures

Swimming differs from other sports in that energy must be used to keep the body in a buoyant, streamlined position. In addition, as the swimmer is attempting to biomechanically propel him- or herself in a horizontal plane, drag forces are attempting to hold the body back, which also uses extra energy. As a rule of thumb, swimming requires four times more energy than running the same distance.

Body fat, which is more buoyant than muscle tissue, gives females an advantage in the water environment. With more fat in the lower body, women have a greater lift in the water and actually experience float rather than drag. With this natural efficiency, women swimmers can cover a given distance using less energy expenditure than men.

Calories are units that measure the amount of energy needed to perform a given task as well as the amount of energy contained in foods. The average male doing little exercise uses 2,800 calories per day, while the average female with a similar lifestyle uses 2,000 calories per day. Active recreational or advanced swimmers may require 4,000 to 5,000 calories per day just to keep even with the calories they expend. At the elite competitive level, this calorie consumption may go as high as 6,000 to 7,000 calories per day.

Swimming a high-intensity freestyle event expends about 9 to 12 calories per minute, while swimming easy freestyle laps takes only about 7 to 9 calories per minute. Measuring caloric expenditure is fairly imprecise because so much depends on the athlete's body weight and swimming ability as well as the intensity, duration, frequency, and strokes used in the swimming session.

To determine the number of calories expended, multiply the number of swimming sessions per week times the length of each session times the approximate intensity of the workout. This might be:

5 sessions per week × 60 minutes per session × 10 calories =
3,000 calories expended per week

Another method of monitoring calories is to do regular weigh-ins. Recorded in the training diary, this gives a good comparison of weight variations and hence calorie expenditure.

Dividing the amount of calories among the three energy sources produces a balanced intake. It should be 10 to 15 percent protein, 25 to 30 percent fat, and 55 to 60 percent carbohydrates.

Protein 10–15%
Fat 25–30% 100% of calories
Carbohydrates 55–60%

In cases where an athlete is expending 5,000 to 7,000 calories per day or for ultradistance swimmers, carbohydrate intake may be increased by 5 to 10 percent. At the same time, fat intake should be decreased slightly.

Athletes who want to gain or lose weight need to adjust calorie intake to produce this result. For most people, even athletes, reducing or maintaining an adequate weight is the main goal. Some people are predisposed to fat accumulation; others have been conditioned to diets that are heavy in fats, creams, and sugars. In addition, all of us are subject to weight gain as we grow older, because the metabolism slows down with age and often there is a reduction in activity as well. One rule to counter this is to reduce calories by approximately 5 percent for every 10 years past the age of 20.

For a weight reduction program, the most effective and realistic goal is a loss of 1 to 2 pounds per week. One pound of fat is the equivalent of 3,500 calories. That means the athlete must eat that many fewer calories or expend that many more in exercise.

Through diet, this can be done by eating 500 fewer calories per day (500 × 7 = 3,500). Initially, diet weight loss is from fluid elimination and some depletion of glycogen. Staying on a low-calorie diet, however, eventually results in loss of fat and muscle tissue. This is a slow, methodical process that requires calorie counting. One-food diets, liquid and pill supplements, starvation, and other fad approaches should be avoided because usually they are not only a health risk, they don't work.

Weight loss can also be accomplished by exercising. This means swimming the 400 to 700 calories away, which requires at least 1 hour of training per day. Most of this weight loss would be from fat tissue.

The best weight-loss method, of course, is a combination of diet and exercise. Through this method, more muscle tissue is maintained while more fat tissue is lost. But, once an adequate training weight is established, a loss of more than 2 to 3 pounds per week may indicate a loss in muscle tissue, which is not desirable.

Gaining weight is accomplished by increasing the amount of

calories in the diet in conjunction with resistance exercise. To gain 1 pound of muscle requires an additional 2,000 to 2,500 calories beyond the amount being used for exercise. To accomplish this, maintain the nutrient percentages, but increase the daily amount and number of servings of the basic foods. A gradual weight gain program is suggested. For example, to gain approximately one pound per week, increase the caloric intake by 350 calories per day.

When an athlete reaches his or her ideal body weight, this should be recorded in the training diary. When optimal performance is in the offing, this weight should be reached and maintained.

Nutritional Needs and Variations

Athletes should eat 3 to 4 hours before a competitive event—this is an individual preference—to prevent hunger and maintain energy levels. This meal should consist of complex carbohydrates and fluids, either water or diluted fruit juice. Stay away from fats, proteins, fried foods, and carbonated drinks. A light, simple meal will not upset the stomach and will be easy to digest without gas or bloating.

Do not consume large amounts of simple sugars (candy or sweet drinks) within 1 hour of the competition. These foods can cause a temporary rise in blood sugar that can result in an upset stomach or diarrhea. Up to 30 or 40 minutes before the competition, drink water or diluted fruit juice if you feel thirsty. Once you determine a satisfactory precompetition diet, record it in your training diary for future reference.

Caffeine is believed to be beneficial to athletes just before endurance competitions because it may cause a mobilization of free fatty acids that can be used for energy before the stored glycogen. Some athletes drink two cups of coffee or tea about 1 hour before the event, but the amount is an individual matter dependent on the athlete's body size. Too much caffeine can cause an increase in heart rate and elevated emotional levels as well as fluid loss through urination. While drinking coffee or tea is accepted in most sports competitions, the International Olympic Committee has banned excessive caffeine use.

Carbohydrate loading is a dietary practice that is being used by athletes who compete in continuous endurance events that last 60 to 90 minutes or more. By eating large quantities of carbohydrates, the muscle glycogen is increased 2 to 3 times above normal values. As the glycogen is consumed during competition, there is more available for the working muscles.

The loading procedure starts 1 week before the competition. The first day, after a long, hard workout, an athlete eats a regular diet. The workout of this day sets up the mechanics for the loading because the glycogen is depleted from the specific muscles that will be used in the competition. In other words, a swimmer should swim, not play racquetball or run for training. For the next 3 days, the athlete does moderate training of the specific muscles for competition and eats a regular diet. The last 3 days should be fairly restful, with little or no training, but the diet is changed to very large quantities of carbohydrates. By the day of the competition, the body has increased stores of carbohydrates.

This method is fairly extreme and, for swimmers just getting into competitive events, should be undertaken only with the approval of a trainer or physician. At most, it should be done only two or three times per year.

A modified 4-day carbo-loading regimen is gaining popularity among athletes. In this version, the athlete does moderate training of specific muscle groups during the first and second days, but eats meals that are high in carbohydrates. The third day is for rest, with high carbohydrate meals. The fourth day is competition day, and the glycogen storage, while not as high as it would be on the 7-day method, is higher than normal. However, this method is more convenient and practical than the 7-day method and probably produces enough increase in glycogen for the competition at hand.

Vegetarians as a group are increasing among the general population as well as among athletes. Eating large amounts of complex carbohydrates is not difficult for them, but vegetarian athletes should be sure that they get adequate protein and fats in the diet. Legumes (dried beans, peas, lentils, peanuts), nuts, and seeds are good sources of protein, and dairy products and eggs also provide protein and fats. It is important to deliberately eat those kinds of foods in addition to carbohydrates to be sure that the diet is well balanced.

Which brings this chapter on eating correctly to a full circle.

Efficient swimming is dependent on energy, and the source of energy is food. But not just any food. A well-balanced diet is essential to the development of the athlete who is efficient in his or her sport.

CHAPTER 10

STAYING HEALTHY

Modern training methods, which are more specific and more demanding than those of the past, place great physical stress on the exercising body. This means that athletes have to be especially aware of weak areas of their bodies, of past injuries, of the prevention of injuries during training and competition, and, not least important, of ways to rehabilitate the body after an injury occurs.

Fortunately, the technology involved in sportsmedicine has made major advances in recent decades that aid athletes in accomplishing these goals. Therapists can advise athletes in the use of training equipment to strengthen weak areas. For the treatment of injuries, there is very sophisticated equipment to provide relief and even heal an injury. Surgical techniques are available that make it possible for athletes to return to training or competition after a very short time. Some surgery can stabilize and enhance the use of a joint or limb after an injury. And much more is known about rehabilitation processes than was ever imagined in the past.

Even with this increase in the knowledge of injury mechanisms, swimmers who are working hard at their sport remain vulnerable to an assortment of injuries that may be acute or chronic. If an injury should occur, or if you have a problem of long duration, the first thing to do is to see a physician who specializes in sportsmedicine. He or she can examine the current injury as well as check preexisting injuries. From this examination, the doctor can provide advice about returning to exercise or limiting training, if necessary.

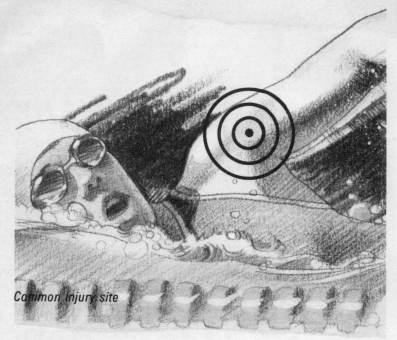

Common injury site

Obviously, it is not necessary to see a doctor for every minor stress experienced in a sport, but self-help techniques derived from reading or inexpert advisers should be avoided. **When an injury seems serious or if pain persists, seek professional advice.** Even the advice provided in this book is not intended to replace informed help, but rather to provide background so that you can make correct judgments about injury prevention and care.

Prevention, of course, is the first step in the continuous process of maintaining a healthy body. Correct training procedures that move at a steady, gradual pace through flexibility, strength, and cardiovascular conditioning exercises are the surest way to avoid injury in the first place.

Preventing Injuries

Weak parts of the body, whether caused by a previous injury or by lack of use, are naturally predisposed to injury, but they are also particularly vulnerable in people who are vigorously pursuing a sport. Where there is a functional imbalance, an athlete should train to build up the weak part. This means making sure not only that the arms and shoulders are equally strong, but that the total body is conditioned for flexibility, strength, and cardiovascular needs. The butterfly stroke, for example, requires emphasis not only on the muscles of the upper and middle back but on those of the shoulders and chest.

The main principles of training—frequency, intensity, duration—require a progressive, gradual build-up. This gradual change of pace allows the body to adapt to new stresses without injury, although there may be mild discomfort when increasing any aspect of training.

The design of a training program must fit each individual athlete like a stretch bathing suit. The program should not have goals that are physically or mentally too demanding, nor should it be rigidly fixed and unchanging if change is needed. Overtraining can result from an athlete's setting unrealistic goals, copying a training program used by another athlete, or competing with a friend during exercise sessions. This can cause stress and lead to injury. Consult a coach or trainer if a training program seems overly demanding. Also be sure that rest periods are included in the training program, to allow your body to recover from the stress of workouts.

Good nutrition is required for the day-to-day building and repair of muscle tissue. This is especially true after an injury, when growth and repair are critical.

Swimming Injuries

Swimming involves large and small muscle group activity to perform repetitive movements at the shoulder, elbow, hip, knee, and ankle joints. Injuries can occur at these spots because of inadequate pre-season training, improper stroke or kick technique, inadequate warm-ups for the speed and power of the workout, too many sets and repetitions at too great an intensity level, inadequate rest periods, or overtraining.

In addition to recognizing these general causes of swimming injuries, athletes need to be aware of technique faults that can cause injuries to specific parts of the body.

Head and neck. Swimming is not a sport in which impact

injuries occur often, but a mistimed freestyle or backstroke closed (flip) turn can result in hitting the head or neck on the wall of the pool. Also, muscles surrounding or leading into the neck, particularly the trapezius and the levator scapulae, can go into spasm or be strained or stretched from repositioning the head in the water during the butterfly recovery. Stroke and breathing patterns can also strain the neck if they are done incorrectly over a long period of time.

Shoulders. The most prevalent swimming injuries occur at the shoulder joints. These injuries include sprains (a stretch or tear of a ligament), strains (a stretch or tear of a muscle or tendon), bursitis (an inflammation of the cushioning joint bursa sac), tendinitis (an inflammation of a muscle tendon), arthritis (general inflammation of joints), and degenerative injuries from overuse. Well developed and balanced shoulder muscles surrounding the joints can help prevent most of those injuries. Stretching of ligaments and tendons surrounding the shoulder joint can also occur from continual use. If it is severe, a swimmer may have to stop swimming to allow the shoulder to heal. If symptoms persist, see a sportsmedicine orthopedist.

Elbows. Tendinitis and muscle spasms at the elbow joint sometimes occur. Usually these problems are due to poor conditioning or improper stroke technique.

Wrists and hands. Impact injuries can occur from hitting the wrist or hand on the wall during turns. These may be abrasions (scraping or friction produced by rubbing motions on the outer layer of skin) or a dislocation (a displacement of bones from the joint capsule, particularly fingers).

Back. Muscle strains and spasms in the upper- and mid-back regions occur frequently among swimmers. The lower back may also experience stress in the butterfly stroke. (The new "head-bobbing" breaststroke tends to hyperextend the back.) Swimmers with preexisting or new back problems should see a doctor for help.

Hips and groin. The most common problems to this region are tendinitis, bursitis, muscle strains, and sciatica (a nerve impingement affecting the sciatic nerve of the buttocks). In the breaststroke, the whip kick is usually the cause of groin injuries, while in the butterfly the dolphin kick can affect the hip flexor muscles.

Upper leg. Muscle strains and spasms can occur in this region from improper warm-up and cool-down as well as improper kicking technique.

Knees. The soft tissues and muscles surrounding the knee joints can experience tendinitis, bursitis, ligament sprains, and tendon strains. Frequently, the breaststroke whip kick is the cause.

Ankles and feet. The freestyle flutter kick can cause tendinitis across the top of the ankle joint. Also, the heels can hit the end of the pool during a closed turn, causing severe bruising, swelling, and discomfort.

Miscellaneous injuries. Eye and ear infections are common among swimmers. Swimmers who train outdoors should be aware of sun exposure.

Warning Signs

Muscle soreness and fatigue are the most common physiological responses to an increase in training. At the same time, a healthy body adapts to this stress through gradual lessening of muscle soreness and fatigue. If these signs do not diminish in 24 to 48 hours, look for more serious injuries that may have occurred.

In addition, an athlete should be on the alert for other warning signals that may indicate serious problems. Acute or short-term warning signs that call for professional assistance are:

Pain can be a sharp or dull discomfort.

Swelling is usually the result of an injury. There may be puffiness and tenderness near the site of an injury and the joint may become stiff.

Redness is the body's reaction to an irritation or an injury. There may also be an increase in temperature at the site.

Fatigue lowers the body's resistance and can lead to colds, infections, and injury complications. Fatigue often results from continual workouts without rest periods.

Muscle soreness is a hint that muscles are being stressed beyond their ability to rebuild and repair themselves.

Dizziness and headaches can indicate that the body is not adapting to training stresses, particularly if they occur on a chronic basis. Nutritional, rest, and recovery patterns may not be correct.

Chronic or long-term warning signs usually indicate a more serious injury.

Caring for Injuries

The most effective methods of caring for injuries range from home remedies to the use of very advanced devices found in hospitals and clinics. After pain and discomfort have left an injury site and damaged tissues have been repaired, exercise therapy is also needed to bring that portion of the body back to its normal fitness level.

Minor injuries generally heal themselves without treatment, but if symptoms continue for more than 3 days, it is best to seek professional help. When minor pain or swelling is uncomfortable, these remedies usually bring relief:

Ice applied to the injury for 1 to 3 days can reduce inflammation, swelling, and pain. Using an ice bag, immersing the limb in ice water, or massaging the injured site with ice should be done for 10 to 15 minutes about three times per day.

Heat can be used to promote joint mobility after the initial swelling, inflammation, and pain have left the injury site. Hot pads or packs, immersion in hot water, and massage with skin counter-irritants, such as analgesic creams and lotions, can be used in a manner similar to the ice treatments. Be very careful when applying heat to injured areas to avoid burns to the skin and surrounding tissue. In no case should heat be applied in the early phases of an injury, because this can increase swelling and inflammation.

Massage promotes blood circulation while decreasing pain and discomfort. The conventional massage techniques manipulate muscles, but other types that require treatment from a trained specialist can be used. These include acupressure and trigger-point massage, in which deep pressure is applied to target nerve reflex sites.

Compression of an injured area that continues to swell may help reduce swelling. An elastic wrap or tape is bound around the site. Extreme caution and a very moderate amount of pressure must be used to avoid cutting off blood circulation to the injured area.

Elevation of an injured limb reduces the blood flow to the site and can hold swelling to a minimum.

For serious injuries or when an apparent minor injury does not respond to the simple remedies described above, the athlete should see a physician who specializes in sportsmedicine. After diagnosis, the doctor will recommend appropriate rehabilitation therapy and call upon a sports therapist or athletic trainer to guide the athlete through an exercise program. Part of the rehabilitation may involve devices that help speed recovery such as electrical muscle stimulators, computerized isokinetic muscle strength and endurance machines, hot and cold whirlpools, treadmills and stationary bicycles, ultrasound machines, transcutaneous electrical nerve stimulators, neuromuscular stimulators, neuroprobes, diathermy, and hot and cold applicators. Exercises to build up the injured area should also be done under the direction of a trained therapist. When these are mastered, the athlete can perform them alone in an exercise center or at home using a device like the S.P.O.R.T. Cord.

Athletes are often impatient to get back to their normal routines after an injury, but it is important to follow a prescribed therapy program very closely. When the injury is healed, it is more important than ever to stick with a well-organized training schedule to pursue the goal of efficient swimming.

CHAPTER 11

MENTAL EFFICIENCY

Sports psychology is the newest addition to the serious athlete's repertoire of training aids. Improvements in mental processes and approaches to sports have enabled individual athletes to make great achievements, but the future of this field holds even more promise. Records will be shattered, not only from better training and technique but from the ability to break down psychological barriers that block top performance.

But even among athletes who are not at the record-breaking level, the psychology of being physically active deserves examination. This begins with asking yourself: why are you active, why take up swimming, and why try to improve performance? The answers to those questions probably hinge on the pleasure and satisfaction of the performance itself, but that is only the superficial reason.

Most people find that being physically active relieves tension and stress and mitigates the problems of daily living and working. Sport is play, which is a very satisfactory counterbalance to work. Sport may also be competitive, which can fulfill an athlete's ego and self-esteem. If other aspects of life are hostile or boring, being physically active may relieve those feelings.

Because sports are an optional avocation for most people, the selection of one over another is more of an intrinsic choice than almost any other we make. This means you perform an activity— swimming—because of personal, inner needs such as becoming fit, experiencing joy, looking better, or relieving stress. Such intrinsic motivation for doing something may last longer and be more satisfying than extrinsic motivations for achieving rewards such as fame, money, and recognition.

Goal Setting

For a sport to have structure, meaning, and focus, a participant needs to set goals to achieve. This means setting up an orderly and systematic process with stated objectives along the way to a final goal. Accomplishing these objectives brings satisfaction for the time and effort put into the work of training and competing and provides the motivation to move to the next step. Having objectives also helps in organizing and using time more efficiently to reach an athlete's full potential.

Goals may vary with ability and skill level, but above all they should be realistic. For a new swimmer this might mean asking the advice of a coach or an instructor to set a potential achievement level. With a set of goals in mind, the next step is to put the goals into three time categories: long term, intermediate, and short term.

Maintaining a written record of these time categories helps an athlete stay on track and plan for the future. Beginners may have fairly general objectives, but as an athlete advances, goals become more specific based on past experiences. This self-knowledge is the element that makes goals individual.

Long-term goals. These are ultimate objectives that may be as lofty as making the Olympic team or as specific as winning a master's swim meet for an age group or as personal as improving times for the 200-meter breaststroke; they may be simply to increase cardiovascular fitness or lose 10 pounds or swim well enough to keep up with family members. Once these goals are set and written down, they should be stored for future reference. Periodically you may want to reassess and adjust the long-term goals. And once you have achieved your goals; it is important to set new ones almost immediately.

Intermediate goals. These are targets that are within a planning time frame. You might set them according to the phases of your training program or according to the seasons, but allow at least two to three months to achieve intermediate goals. Keep these goals closer to the front of your mind, and from time to time take a look at them for reevaluation and resetting, if necessary.

Short-term goals. These are the goals that you can see from day to day and week to week. You will need to think and to plan the quality and quantity of workouts based on these goals and determine whether you accomplished the last one or need to work on it more. Keeping a precise and accurate record of workouts helps in assessing short-term goals so that you will be sure to cover the distance or laps, work at the proper intensity, and achieve the times specified.

Mind over Muscles

Skills in sports must be developed to the point where they are as automatic and efficient as walking. The objective is to require so little conscious effort in the mechanics of stroke, kick, and technique that the brain is free to concentrate on other aspects of the race or lap swimming.

Initially, however, learning a new stroke or correcting bad habits may feel awkward and inefficient. This is to be expected because the central nervous system is tense and unsure in learning new patterns. At this stage, conscious effort is required and the strain of such effort often results in more fatiguing workouts than usual. But with practice and repetition the new movements gradually move into the unconscious and result in fluid, relaxed, efficient swimming technique.

The process of learning a sport follows a definite pattern that starts with watching the movements performed correctly, moves on to imitating the movements watched, and then to practicing and repeating those movements over a long period of time. That process is particularly important for less skilled swimmers. Seeing and studying a stroke as it is correctly demonstrated sets a mental goal to achieve. The next step is to imitate the stroke, and here a swimmer may need a coach or an instructor to observe and correct errors. In this part of learning, however, talking about the stroke is not as helpful as doing it. More advanced swimmers may benefit from verbalization and explanation about technique and the nuances of a particular stroke or movement, but at lower ability levels this is time-wasting and confusing.

As you advance in acquiring swimming skills, other approaches can help in achieving goals.

Whole-part-whole. At certain times during training it is helpful to work on specific parts of a stroke or kick by isolating and practicing them exclusively. To do this, devices such as kickboards and pull-buoys are useful. This kind of practice should not, however, become the major thrust of a swimmer's workouts. Total body movement that takes in coordination and timing between the stroke and the kick should be the major emphasis in training.

Speed versus accuracy. Strokes can be practiced in slow motion in order to develop the highest perfection in form. For advanced swimming, however, some practice sets should be at or near maximum pace so that you mentally memorize the feeling of the strokes and kicks. Learning a stroke to perfection at a slow speed will require that you later relearn the timing and coordination at a faster speed. One of the most important concepts in sports science is the law of specificity. Training and practice must be as specific and similar as possible in the environment, pace, intensity, and the way the muscle groups are used.

Learning and fatigue. Should swimming be practiced while a swimmer is tired? If the strokes are to be performed for peak performance or in recreational situations when the swimmer might be fatigued, then yes, learning should take place in similar situations. If a skill has been poorly learned or a bad habit has not been eliminated, such errors will appear during the fatiguing and stressful parts of swimming. In other words, practicing while tired is a rehearsal for the real thing just as practicing while fresh and alert is a rehearsal for the real thing.

Feedback. This is information or a measure of how well you are progressing in learning and improving swimming skills. Feedback might come from a coach, instructor, or training partner. It might be from a video tape of your swimming or a stopwatch measurement of your time. Whatever the source, feedback should be as objective as possible so that you will know how you are doing and make corrections or intensify effort to gain on your goals. To be most effective, feedback should be given immediately after a performance. But to correct errors and improve performance takes time and patience.

Overlearning. This is defined as continually practicing a stroke after it appears to have been learned correctly. How much does a stroke need to be practiced before it is learned—and overlearned?

That is a theoretical question that varies with each individual and his or her ability level, but retention is enhanced when a skill is overlearned. Obviously, this is vital for swimming, which requires repetition over time and distance.

Training times. The scheduling of practice and training sessions has a significant impact on how effectively a swimmer learns. Generally, shorter sessions, spread over a longer period of time, are more effective than one long training session. For example, three 1-hour sessions every other day for a week are better than one 3-hour session per week. This kind of schedule may not be ideal for everyone, but increasing amounts of practice in a short time period will not necessarily result in improved performance. For example, resistance training every day is not as effective as training three times a week with a day of rest between each session.

Variety. Doing the same training week after week can become tedious and boring, often resulting in making an athlete feel tired, unenthusiastic, and discouraged. What has happened is that the athlete has reached a plateau. The only way out of this situation is to change workout routines, add a new stroke to the repertoire, or enter races. Any alteration in the daily routine will break the pattern and provide new short-term goals that offer enhanced motivation.

Style versus technique. The mechanical principles of a swimming stroke are the technique of swimming. This doesn't mean that all swimmers will perform the mechanics in exactly the same way. Limb length and body size, personality, and approach have a large influence on how people swim. This is individual style. Swimmers can borrow mechanical principles from other swimmers, but they can't borrow individual style. That is innate.

Simplicity. Technique analysis needs to be simple. Thinking about every nuance of your stroke while you are swimming is counterproductive and reduces the smooth, fluid performance that is a swimmer's goal. Practice and time will improve the mechanics of the stroke. In competition or during a self-testing period, let the mind concentrate on the simple aspects of performance: start, stroke/kick, turn, and strategy.

Success and Failure

Motivation is the mental fuel that makes a performance go. It has to be combined with practice and training to produce the end product: performance. Learning plus motivation play an integral part in this process.

Success or failure to achieve goals influences an athlete's motivation. Success tends to raise aspiration levels and motivation, while failure tends to lower them. But this is not a black or white equation, either. Constant success makes a task seem too easy and results in boredom. Constant failure produces discouragement and lack of energy. The secret to maintaining motivation is to have a balance between success and failure. To produce this performance fuel, an athlete—even a consistent winner—needs to feel some probability that he or she could fail. On the other hand, an athlete who usually fails should also feel that there is some probability that he or she could win—this time.

One way to manipulate motivation is to alter goals. Goals that are too high or are unattainable can be adjusted to within the realm of possibility. As an example, this means recognizing that not everyone in a race can be the winner, and that those who don't win are not by definition failures. Others in the race may have improved their times, completed their longest distance, or simply finished their first race. On the other hand, goals that are too low can be changed to raise the level of aspiration. Personal time limits can be increased, more difficult meets can be entered, or the type of event can be changed. In this case, the complacency cycle must be broken.

All of this goal manipulation revolves around the athlete's ability to evaluate his or her individual performance. Comparison, yes, but comparison with one's own achievements rather than against those of an Olympic champion. Not everyone can be an elite athlete, but everyone can realize his or her potential in fitness and pleasure.

Anxiety depends on how an athlete perceives an event or task to be performed, which relates directly to past experiences in similar situations. While anxiety needs to be controlled, a total lack of anxiety may be bad for some types of performances. A weight lifter, for instance, needs this mental process to help produce the high level of adrenaline to perform. A piano player, on the other hand, who is doing complex motor tasks, needs to be calm and have reduced anxiety to perform. In swimming, shorter distances require higher degrees of intensity and allow for more anxiety, but too much anxiety can result in a tight, tense performance of inefficient movements. Often, this is called "trying too hard." The athlete ends the race feeling tired and wrung out. What is needed is confidence in one's ability to perform based on past performances.

Mental rehearsal can aid in developing this confidence. To do this an athlete visualizes each part of the workout or race—start, entry into the water, strokes, turns, and strategy—with a positive outcome. Complicated technical aspects of the event are eliminated along with negative thoughts. Such deep concentration, which is essentially racing the event before it happens, requires a few moments of quiet during or after the warm-up period. This mental practice can be more valuable than all your previous water workouts.

Pressure builds up at the time of the race, butterflies in the stomach are normal, the atmosphere is heavy with competition, and the swimmer's mind must handle a variety of outside influences. To deal with this pressure and not permit it to turn into stress, you must have confidence in the training and practice you have done over the past weeks, take an adequate warm-up, previsualize the race, and not try to analyze technique or force skills. At poolside, keep your approach to the meet simple and concentrate on the situation at hand: start, stroke/kick, turn, and strategy. This will make a swimmer ready and confident.

The Sports Process

The moment on the victory podium is equally brief for Olympic champions and for swim-club winners. The time it takes to get to the podium is long. That is why sports training and practice need to be satisfying and fulfilling. This is the part—call it the struggle toward a goal or the process of acquiring skills—that is most meaningful and long remembered by athletes at the top as well as the bottom levels of competition and recreation.

The process is the day-to-day workouts, accomplishing goals, and moving to the next phase in swim training. It is also the friends made, places visited, and experiences encountered through the sport. These are the things, more than the trophies, that make an impact on your life. In the end, the process becomes more important than the ultimate goal. It will always be part of your life and will always be rewarding in itself.

APPENDIX A
Bibliography

Armstrong, R.B. "Mechanisms of Exercise-Induced Delayed Onset Muscular Soreness: A Brief Review. *Medicine and Science in Sports and Exercise* Vol. 16, No. 6, 1984.

Beaulieu, J.E. "Developing a Stretching Program." *The Physician and SportsMedicine* Vol. 9, No. 11, 1981.

Bonner, H.W. "Energy Systems Used During Swimming." *Swimming Technique,* November 1980.

Brooks, G., and T. Fahey. *Exercise Physiology: Human Bioenergetics and Its Applications.* Wiley & Sons, 1984.

Carron, A.V. *Sport Psychology: An Analysis of Athlete Behavior* (motivating the athlete). Mouvement Publications, 1978.

Clark, N. "How I Manage Athletes' Food Obsessions." *The Physician and SportsMedicine* Vol. 12, No. 7, 1984.

————. *The Athlete's Kitchen.* Bantam Books, 1983.

Costill, D.L., W.J. Fink, M. Hargreaves, D.S. King, R. Thomas, and R. Fielding. "Metabolic Characteristics of Skeletal Muscle During Detraining from Competitive Swimming." *Medicine and Science in Sports and Exercise* Vol. 17, No. 3, 1985.

Costill, D.L., W.J. Fink, and M.L. Pollock. "Muscle Fiber Composition and Enzyme Activities of Elite Distance Runners." *Medicine and Science in Sports* No. 8, 1976.

Costill, D.L., D.S. King, R. Thomas, and M. Hargreaves. "Effects of Reduced Training on Muscular Power in Swimmers." *The Physician and SportsMedicine* Vol. 13, No. 2, 1985.

DeVries, H.A. "Evaluation of Static Stretching Procedures for Improvement of Flexibility." *Research Quarterly* No. 33, 1962.

————. *Physiology of Exercise* (3rd ed.). William C. Brown, 1980.

Dominguez, R.H. "Shoulder Pain in Swimmers." *The Physician and SportsMedicine* Vol. 8, No. 7, 1980.

Dummer, G., D.H. Clarke, P. Vaccaro, L. Vander Velden, A.H. Goldfarb, and J. Sockler. "Age-Related Differences in Muscular Strength and Muscular Endurance Among Female Masters Swimmers." *Research Quarterly for Exercise and Sport* Vol. 56, No. 2, 1985.

Fahey, T. *What to Do About Athletic Injuries.* Butterick Publishing, 1979.

Fox, E.L. *Sports Physiology* (2nd ed.). W.B. Saunders, 1985.

Fox, S.M., J.P. Naughton, and P.A. Gorman. "Physical Activity and Cardiovascular Health II. The Exercise Prescription: Intensity and Duration." *Modern Concepts of Cardiovascular Disease* No. 16, 1972.

Garhammer, J. *Sports Illustrated Strength Training.* Harper & Row, 1986.

Grandjean, A.C., editor. *Nutrition for Sport Success.* The American Alliance for Health, Physical Education, Recreation and Dance, Reston, Virginia, 1984.

Greipp, J.F. "Swimmer's Shoulder: The Influence of Flexibility and Weight Training." *The Physician and SportsMedicine* Vol. 13, No. 8, 1985.

Hagerman, F.C. *How to Increase Your Speed and Agility.* Perigee Books, Putnam Publishing, 1986.

Halliwell, W. *Sport Psychology: An Analysis of Athlete Behavior* (intrinsic motivation in sport). Mouvement Publications, 1978.

Haskell, W., J. Scala, and J. Whittam, editors. *Nutrition and Athletic Performance: Proceedings of the Conference on Nutritional Determinants in Athletic Performance.* Bull Publishing, 1982.

Hempel, L.S., and C.L. Wells. "Cardiorespiratory Cost of the Nautilus Express Circuit." *The Physician and SportsMedicine* Vol. 13, No. 4, 1985.

Hickson, J.F., J.H. Wilmore, M.J. Buono, and S.H. Constable. "Energy Cost of Weight Training Exercise." *National Strength and Conditioning Association Journal* Vol. 6, No. 5, 1984.

Jopke, T. "Training Swimmers: How Coaches Get Results." *The Physician and SportsMedicine* Vol. 10, No. 6, 1982.

Katz, J. *Swimming for Total Fitness.* Doubleday & Co., 1981.

Lawther, J.D. *Sport Psychology: An Analysis of Athlete Behavior* (developmental stages for motivation in sport). Mouvement Publications, 1978.

Loucks, A.B., and S.M. Horvath. "Athletic Amenorrhea: A Review." *Medicine and Science in Sports and Exercise* Vol. 17, No. 1, 1985.

Maglischo, E.W. *Swimming Faster.* Mayfield Publishing, 1982.

McArdle, W.D., F.I. Katch, and V.L. Katch. *Exercise Physiology: Energy, Nutrition, and Human Performance.* Lea & Febiger, 1981.

Mickelson, T., and F.C. Hagerman. "Warm-up, Warm-down." *The Oarsman,* Jan.–Feb. 1978.

Moffroid, M.T., and R.H. Whipple. "Specificity of Speed of Exercise." *Physical Therapy* No. 50, 1970.

Moore, M. "Carbohydrate Loading: Eating Through the Wall." *The Physician and SportsMedicine* Vol. 9, No. 10, 1981.

National Dairy Council. *Food Power: A Coach's Guide to Improving Performance.* Rosemont, Illinois, 1983.

National Strength and Conditioning Association: Roundtable. "Determining Factors of Strength, I." *National Strength and Conditioning Association Journal* Vol. 7, No. 1, 1985.

National Strength and Conditioning Association: Roundtable. "Determining Factors of Strength, II." *National Strength and Conditioning Association Journal* Vol. 7, No. 2, 1985.

National Strength and Conditioning Association: Roundtable. "Strength Training and Conditioning for the Female Athlete." *Strength and Conditioning Association Journal* Vol. 7, No. 3, 1985.

O'Shea, J.P. *Scientific Principles and Methods of Strength Fitness* (2nd ed.). Addison-Wesley, 1976.

Pearl, B. *Keys to the Universe.* Bill Pearl Enterprises, 1982.

Pollock, M.L., J.H. Wilmore, and S.M. Fox III. *Exercise in Health and Disease.* W.B. Saunders, 1984.

Prentice, W.E. "A Comparison of Static Stretching and PNF Stretching for Improving Hip Joint Flexibility." *Athletic Training* 18(1), 1983.

Prins, J. "Overdistance: Training the Aerobic Systems." *Swimming Technique,* November 1980.

Roy, S., and R. Irvin. *Sports Medicine: Prevention, Evaluation, Management, and Rehabilitation.* Prentice-Hall, 1983.

Rushall, B.S. *Some Applications of Psychology to Swimming.* Sixth Annual Illinois Swimming Association Clinic, 1970–71.

Sapega, A.A., T.C. Quedenfeld, and R.A. Moyer. "Biophysical Factors in Range-of-Motion Exercise." *The Physician and SportsMedicine* Vol. 9, No. 12, 1981.

Schulz, S., and S. Rodeo. "Stanford University Dryland Training Program." *National Strength and Conditioning Association Journal* Vol. 6, No. 2, 1984.

Schwane, J.A., B.G. Watrous, S.R. Johnson, and R.B. Armstrong. "Is Lactic Acid Related to Delayed-Onset Muscle Soreness?" *The Physician and SportsMedicine* Vol. 11, No. 3, 1983.

Sharkey, B.J. *Physiology of Fitness* (2nd ed.). Human Kinetics Publishers, 1984.

Sharp, R.L., and D.L. Costill. "Force, Work, and Power: What They Mean to the Competitive Swimmer." *Swimming World* No. 23, 1982.

Sharp, R.L., J.P. Troup, and D.L. Costill. "Relationship Between Power and Sprint Freestyle Swimming." *Medicine and Science in Sports and Exercise* Vol. 14, No. 1, 1982.

Shellock, F. "Physiological Benefits of Warm-up." *The Physician and SportsMedicine* Vol. 11, No. 10, 1983.

Singer, R.N. *Motor Learning and Human Performance*. Macmillan, 1968.

———. *Coaching, Athletics, and Psychology*. McGraw-Hill, 1972.

———. "Sports Psychology: Waves of the Future." *The Physician and SportsMedicine* Vol. 9, No. 3, 1981.

———. "Thought Processes and Emotions in Sport." *The Physician and SportsMedicine* Vol. 10, No. 7, 1982.

Skinner, J.S., and T.H. McLellan. "The Transition from Aerobic to Anaerobic Metabolism." *Research Quarterly for Exercise and Sport* Vol. 51, No. 1, 1980.

Slavin, J.L., and D.J. Joensen. "Caffeine and Sports Performance." *The Physician and SportsMedicine* Vol. 13, No. 5, 1985.

Smith, N.J. *Food for Sport*. Bull Publishing, 1976.

Stamford, B. "The Difference Between Strength and Power (Sportsmedicine adviser)." *The Physician and SportsMedicine* Vol. 13, No. 7, 1985.

———. "Flexibility and Stretching (Sportsmedicine adviser)." *The Physician and SportsMedicine* Vol. 12, No. 2, 1984.

Stone, M.H., H. O'Bryant, J. Garhammer, J. McMillan, and R. Rozenek. "A Theoretical Model of Strength Training." *National Strength and Conditioning Association Journal* Vol. 4, No. 4, 1982.

Straub, W.F., editor. *Sport Psychology: An Analysis of Athlete Behavior.* Mouvement Publications, 1978.

Troup, J.M., Plyley, R. Sharp, and D.L. Costill. "Development of Peak Performance: Strength Training and Tapering." *Swimming World,* August 1981.

Tutko, T.A., and J.W. Richards. *Psychology of Coaching.* Allyn & Bacon, 1971.

Vaccaro, P., G.M. Dummer, and D.H. Clarke. "Physiological Characteristics of Female Masters Swimmers." *The Physician and SportsMedicine* Vol. 9, No. 12, 1981.

Wells, C.L., and S.A. Plowman. "Sexual Differences in Athletic Performance: Biological or Behavioral?" *The Physician and SportsMedicine* Vol. 11, No. 8, 1983.

Wells, K.F., and K. Luttgens. *Kinesiology* (6th ed.). W.B. Saunders, 1976.

Williams, M.H. *Nutrition for Fitness and Sport.* William C. Brown, 1983.

Wilmore, J.H. "Assessing the Swimmer's Body Composition." *Swimming World,* December 1979.

APPENDIX B

SWIMMING
INFORMATION

Swim Magazine
PO Box 2168
Simi Valley, CA 93062
805-527-2708

Triathlon Federation/USA
PO Box 1963
Davis, CA 95617-1963
916-757-2831

United States Masters Swimming, Inc.
5 Tigott Lane
Avon, CT 06001
203-677-9464

United States Swimming, Inc.
1750 E. Boulder St.
Colorado Springs, CO 80909
303-578-4578